COMPOSITION
&WOOD
Dolls and Toys
A Collector's Reference Guide

COMPOSITION
&WOOD

Dolls and Toys
A Collector's Reference Guide

by Michele Karl

ANTIQUE TRADER BOOKS
A Division of
Landmark Specialty Publications
Norfolk, Virginia

ISBN: 0-930625-92-7
Library of Congress Catalog Card Number: 98-71059

Editor: Sandra Holcombe
Editorial Assistant: Wendy Chia-Klesch
Designers: Chris Decker & Heather Ealey
Cover Design: Heather Ealey

Printed in the United States of America

The monetary values in this book should be used as a guide only. Prices vary depending on the area of the country, condition, and supply and demand. This book is a guide and is not intended to set prices. Neither the author nor the publisher assumes responsibility for losses that might be incurred as a result of using this book and its prices.

To order additional copies of this book, or to obtain a catalog, please contact:
Antique Trader Books
P.O. Box 1050
Dubuque, Iowa 52004
or call 1-800-334-7165

Cover Photos: Jaymar Giraffe (top right); Kohner Brothers Pull Toy (top left); Ideal's Shirley Temple with original box (left), Courtesy of Susan Killoran; Pinocchio, Jiminy Cricket, and Figaro (center), Author's Collection; Toby Character Doll (center bottom), Author's Collection; Madame Alexander's Scarlett O'Hara (right), Courtesy of Pat Wood.

TABLE OF CONTENTS

Chapter 1   The Cameo Doll Company & Joseph Kallus 8

Chapter 2   Character Dolls & Toys 26

Chapter 3   Disney Dolls & Toys 40

Chapter 4   Black Composition Dolls 52

Chapter 5   The Effanbee Doll Company & The Patsy Family 60

Chapter 6   Hustler Toy Company 76

Chapter 7   The Ideal Toy Corporation & The Shirley Temple Dolls 82

Chapter 8   Jaymar Specialty Company 100

Chapter 9   Kohner Brothers 116

Chapter 10   Madame Alexander Doll Company & The Dionne Quintuplets 126

Chapter 11   Schoenhut Dolls & Toys 156

Chapter 12   Ted Toyler Inc. 172

Chapter 13   Unmarked Dolls 180

Chapter 14   Some of the Rest 198

ACKNOWLEDGMENTS

I want to acknowledge my husband Joe—every woman should be so lucky to have a guy like this one. His patience, understanding, love, devotion, and—most of all—his support helped me complete this project. To Oscar Kronick for his wonderful photography and allowing me to drag him all over photographing dolls and toys. (More than fifty percent of the photos in this book were shot by Oscar.) For allowing me to take photos of their collections, and giving me photos, ads, and background information on their collections, I'd like to thank Keith Schneider and Liz Cormier of Gasoline Alley in Seattle, Washington; Sharron's Dolls in Ryderwood, Washington; Elisabeth Burdon from Nineteenth Century Imprints in Portland, Oregon; Keith from Irene's Archives in Everett, Washington; James & Judy Sneed of Hollywood, South Carolina, who sent me a great selection of photographs on wood toys and Schoenhut Circus pieces; Annette's Antique Dolls in Bellingham, Washington; Dan Sumpter for his wonderful Jaymar photographs; Jim & Tom Skahill of Jesco Corporation for letting me search through files on the Cameo Doll Company, and for their input; Ronnie Kauk for her Kohner photographs; Robert Greene for his great selection of wood jointed doll photographs; McMaster's Doll Auctions in Cambridge, Ohio; Cobb's Doll Auctions in Johnstown, Ohio; Christie's Images in New York, New York; Judd Lawson in Seattle, Washington; Carl Kludt in Tacoma, Washington; Annette's Antique Dolls in Bellingham, Washington; the Madame Alexander Doll Company; the Effanbee Doll Company; and Vicki Lane of Mercer Island, Washington. For welcoming me into their homes and sharing their collections, I'd like to thank Pat Wood of Battleground, Washington; Susan Killoran of Burien, Washington; and Lennae Ramsey of Gresham, Oregon. And, last but not least, to my mom, Sunnie Newell, from Portland, Oregon, for sharing her collection and her love of dolls with me.

INTRODUCTION

Composition dolls are those made of sawdust mixed with glue. This paste-like mixture is placed into heated, two-piece molds, allowing the doll to be both molded and properly dried in a single process. The dolls are then sanded, painted, and assembled.

I have been a collector for as long as I can remember. Growing up as a "pack-rat," I seemed to have collected just about everything! Dolls and toys have always been my true love. Drawn to the composition and wood types, I searched for a book that included the types of items I collected. The only books I could find had bits and pieces of information, but nowhere was there a book on the subject as a whole. That's when the decision was made to start on this project. After over one year's worth of researching and taking/gathering photographs, *Composition & Wood Dolls and Toys* is ready for your perusal. Enjoy the wonderful photographs and if you're not a collector now, I'm sure you'll want to start when you see what's available.

HOW TO USE THIS BOOK

The various companies are listed in alphabetical order. Many of the items fall into more than one category. For instance, Snow White can be found in Chapter 2, "Character Dolls & Toys," and in Chapter 10, "Madame Alexander Doll Company & The Dionne Quintuplets," though the photo may only be pictured in one place. (Check the index for specific items.) This book is meant to help you identify the dolls and toys listed. Prices are based on several factors, including condition, rarity, size, and availability—and were determined by sales from shows, auctions, retail outlets, and ads. Remember that prices may vary from area to area, and are intended only as a guide. Also, the prices listed are for mint dolls with original clothing—dolls not in mint condition and with replaced clothing can lower their value by fifty percent. Every attempt has been made to make sure all information is accurate.

Chapter One
The Cameo Doll Company & Joseph Kallus

Those of you who are already familiar with the work of Joseph Kallus will find this to be a very exciting chapter. Included are wonderful examples of his work, such as never-before-published photographs of two of his designs. If you aren't familiar with Mr. Kallus's work, this will introduce you to one of the most talented doll designers and manufacturers of this time. Sure, I sound a little prejudiced, but that's because my collection contains many of his designs, and I love his work. He is, by far, one of my favorite doll designers. I think you'll be happy with the examples you'll see in this chapter.

Joseph Kallus met Rose O'Neill, the original designer of the Kewpie Doll, at the meek age of seventeen. He was a student, studying art at the Pratt Institute, when he was selected by Rose O'Neill to work on the "Kewpie Project." Mrs. O'Neill had obtained a copyright in 1913 for the Kewpie, which she had been selling for advertisements and drawings. Mrs. O'Neill needed help marketing the Kewpies. In 1912, just before a patent

was obtained, she met with a company that was interested in marketing the Kewpies as dolls and figurines. That company was Geo. Borgfeldt & Co. of New York. Students who could draw children were asked to show their work to Fred Kolb, of Borgfeldt, who was developing a line of Kewpie novelties. Joseph Kallus beat out the crowd, and so began the relationship with Rose O'Neill and the beginning of Joseph Kallus's doll designing days. In 1916, Joseph Kallus founded the Rex Company, a firm that produced composition dolls—including the Kewpies. Kallus kept a close relationship

Joseph Kallus with a collection of Kewpie Dolls. Courtesy of Jesco Corporation.

with the Geo. Borgfeldt Company, which was the distributor for the dolls. He also had a brief association with the Mutual Doll Company from 1918 until about 1921. This company manufactured Kewpies and Baby Bundie. Rose O'Neill designed several dolls for the Cameo Doll Co., which was founded by Joseph Kallus in 1922. Many of the pieces designed were made using a combination of wood and composition. Joseph Kallus used many original designs for his dolls. Other dolls were interpretations of different artists' designs. Besides making dolls for his company, he made doll heads for other companies, including the Ideal Toy Corporation.

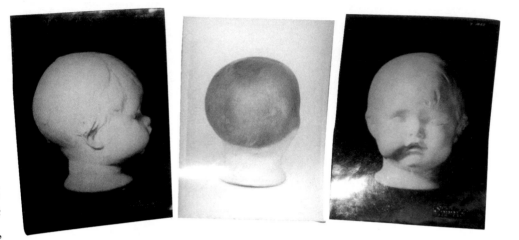

Joseph Kallus designed a myriad of dolls over his working years from 1912 well into the 1960s. In 1970, the Jesco Corporation, based in California, was granted many of the copyrights and patents of the Cameo Doll Company's dolls.

Jesco, in turn, licensed the rights to produce Kewpie to the Rose Art Company in 1993. Production of the Kewpies was geared toward children's play dolls, and not collector dolls. Rose Art produced Kewpies in 1994 and 1995. The company did not produce Kewpie or any other of the original Cameo dolls in the entire year of 1996. Jesco Corporation is working on bringing Kewpie back in the near future for collectors and children, young and old, to enjoy.

Many of the records from the early years of the Cameo Doll Company were lost or destroyed in a fire, making it nearly impossible to exactly identify some of the dates of produced pieces. The dates given for the dolls are the copyright dates rather than the production dates. Many pieces were copyrighted, but not put into production for one to several years later. One example is Popeye, who was copyrighted by King Features Syndicate in 1932, but not produced until 1935.

Cameo Doll Company photos of a mold for the Baby Bo-Kaye head. Courtesy of Jesco Corp.

A wonderful Rose O'Neill drawing of a Kewpie with the Cameo logo.

Portrait of Joseph Kallus.
Courtesy of Jesco Corp.

Three pictures of Joy out of the Cameo catalog.

Close-up of face plates for Cameo Dolls.

Three photos of Marcia from the Cameo catalog.

A wonderful grouping of Bimbo, Pete the Pup, and Betty Boop
from the Cameo catalog.

Above and above right: Rare photos of a prototype for a Sailor. The patent for this doll was denied, and neither the Baseball Player at right nor the Sailor were ever produced. This is the first time photos of this doll have been published.

Right: VERY RARE photo of a prototype for a Baseball Player that is wood jointed. The patent for this doll was denied. This is the first time a photo of this doll has been published.

Both dolls designed by Joseph Kallus.

THE FOLLOWING LIST INCLUDES THE DOLLS
JOSEPH KALLUS DESIGNED, ALONG WITH DATES.

BABY BUNDIE—1918

BO-FAIR—1919

BABY BO-KAYE—1925

BABY BLOSSOM—1927

BABY SNOOKS (FANNY BRICE)—1939

BANDY (BANDMASTER)—EARLY 1930S

BETTY BOOP—1932

BIMBO—*BETTY BOOP'S DOG*

BONZO (THE DOG)—1928

CAT—1930S

CHAMP—1942

CROWNIE—1940

DOG—1930S

DOLLIE—1921

DUMBO—1942

FELIX THE CAT—1928

GIGGLES—1946

GINGER, BONES, & STREAK—1930

HOTPOINT MAN—DATE UNKNOWN

HOWDY DOODY—1947

JEEP—1942

JIMINY CRICKET—1940

JOY—1932

LITTLE ANNIE ROONEY—1925

LITTLE KING—1939

MARCIA—1933

MARGIE—1929

MICKEY MOUSE—1930S

MR. PEANUT—1935

PETE THE PUP—1932

PINKIE—1930

PINOCCHIO—1940

POPEYE—1935

RCA RADIOTRON—1930

SANTA—1935

SISSIE—1928

SUPERMAN—LATE 1940S

TIMOTHY MOUSE—1942

VANITIE—1921

BABY BO-KAYE—1925
Composition head, cloth body, composition arms and legs (also made with bisque or celluloid head); composition, 18", $450-$600; bisque, fully jointed 5", $1,000-$1,250; 6", $1,400-$1,600; 17"-19", $2,500-$3,000; celluloid head, 15"-16", $450-$600. Composition heads by Cameo Doll Co. Bisque heads by Alt, Beck & Gottschalack. Bodies by K & K Toy Co., New York. Distributed by Geo. Borgfeldt Co., NY.

BABY BLOSSOM—1927
Composition head, curved arms, legs, cloth body. Similar to the Effanbee Bubbles, opened mouth, two teeth showing, cloth body, sleep eyes, 20", $575 and up. Courtesy of Lynnae Ramsey.

BANDY (BANDMASTER)—EARLY 1930S
Bandy was produced for GE (General Electric) as an advertising gimmick for the Christmas holiday season. The name Bandy, which is short for Bandmaster, came as a title used for GE's "Bandwagon Campaign" for the company's radio department. This photo shows the baton in both hands. Composition head, wood-segmented body, with bandmaster's hat and stick in hand, 18", $1,000-$1,500. Author's Collection.

BETTY BOOP—1932
Betty was a popular cartoon character, along with her dog, Bimbo. Composition head, wood-segmented arms & legs, molded composition torso, 12", $750-$1,000. Courtesy of Carl Kludt.

BIMBO—
BETTY BOOP'S
DOG
Bimbo is 7 1/2", wood-jointed with composition head and body, painted features, leather ears, $750-$1,000. Courtesy of Annette's Antique Dolls.

This is a reproduction of the Betty Boop Doll. Molds are available today to reproduce her; however, the entire doll is made out of a composition base with no wood-jointed parts. Made by Anne Fosnot, $75-$100.

CAT—1930S
Cameo Cat made with a composition head and wood-jointed body, painted features, leather ears, 7 1/2", $350-$500. Courtesy of Robert Greene.

CROWNIE—1940
Joseph Kallus's drawings of Crownie. Composition head, wood-segmented body; king character with crown, $1,000 and up. A very rare piece. Courtesy of Jesco Corp.

DUMBO—1942
Composition with painted red hands, white toes; yellow composition hat on top with large felt ears; marked "Cameo Dumbo c. WDP." Head and trunk jointed, a Walt Disney design, 8 1/2"-9", $550-$750. Courtesy of Robert Greene.

DOG—1930S
This photo shows an unmarked dog that was made in different colors by the Cameo Doll Company. He's 7 1/4" high and 11" long, molded composition with painted features. His legs are jointed to move when pulled by string. Very unusual piece, $200-$250. Courtesy of Robert Greene.

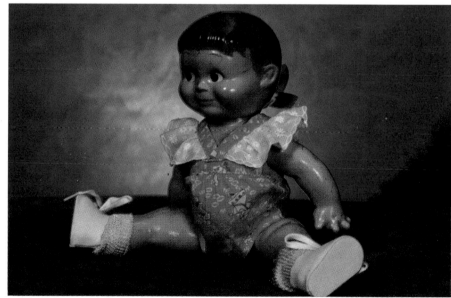

FELIX THE CAT—1928
All wood segments jointed with elastic, 3 1/2", $200; 8 1/2", $300-$350; 13", $375-$500. Felix was copyrighted by Pat Sullivan. Wood-jointed Felixes were also produced by the Schoenhut Company. This Felix uses the composition and wood-jointed body with a vinyl head. 9", $250-$395. Courtesy of Robert Greene.

GIGGLES—1946
The Giggles pictured above is composition, jointed at neck, hips, and shoulders. She is 14" tall, unmarked, with painted features, molded hair, and a slit to attach ribbon. Designed by Rose O'Neill. Other fully jointed, all-composition Giggles dolls, with a molded hair loop for bow, and molded bangs, were also made in 12", 13", and 14" versions, $450-$575. Author's Collection.

STREAK—1930
Streak is wood-jointed with a composition molded head, painted features, and a collar that reads, "Streak." Painted brown, it's one of three dogs (Bones and Ginger are the other two) of this nature produced by the Cameo Doll Company, 7" high, 8" long, $250-$375. Courtesy of Robert Greene.

HOTPOINT MAN
According to William Longstreet, whose father worked for the Hotpoint Company for over 20 years, the Hotpoint Man was known as "Happy Hotpoint." He was used as an advertising gimmick for Hotpoint Appliance. Foot is marked "Cameo Doll Company." Here is a front view of "Happy Hotpoint," 16", all composition with molded head and painted features, original decal on chest, $1,000-$1,500. Author's Collection.

JOY—1932
Beautiful example of Joy, with molded head and space for a ribbon to run through her hair, composition head and body with original label on chest, painted features, wood-jointed arms and legs with shoes painted blue, 10", $225-$300; 15", $325-$500. Author's Collection.

Right: Advertising piece for Happy Hotpoint. Courtesy of Irene's Archives.

JEEP—1942
Popeye's Dog, composition and wood-segmented tail, fully jointed, licensed by King Features Syndicate, 7 1/4", 9", 12 1/2", $595-$995.

By viewing all three sizes of Jeep, you can notice slight differences in their appearance. Note that the body on the 6" Jeep and 8" Jeep are two pieces, while the 12" Jeep uses a one-piece body. Also, the arms and legs on the larger version are one piece and the feet are painted with red spots. Courtesy of Robert Greene.

A color photograph of Howdy Doody is featured on page 84 in Chapter 7.

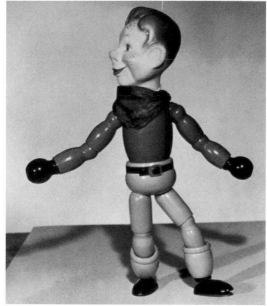

Original Cameo Company photograph of Howdy Doody.

HOWDY DOODY—1947
Made by the Effanbee Doll Company, which—at the time—was owned by Nora Electric, a Christmas tree light manufacturer. Composition head; jointed, wood-segmented body; 13", $500-$750.

LITTLE KING—1940
Composition with wood-jointed arms and legs,
jointed at shoulder, decal on chest, cape behind,
12", $450-$600. Courtesy of Irene's Archives.
Designed by Joseph Kallus, made by Ideal.

MARGIE—1929
Composition head, wood-segmented body, 5"-6",
$195-$250; 10", $200-$295; 15", $275-$350;
19", $350-$400.

MARCIA—1933
All composition girl with molded hair, painted
features, eyes looking off to one side, molded and
painted shoes and socks, French-styled clothing,
$595 and up. Marcia with five-piece composition
body, sleep eyes, mohair wig, $375 and up.

Photo from the Cameo Doll Company catalog
showing Marcia with three different outfits.

Immediate Left: A hard-to-find Margie, 19". But,
is she really a Margie? She looks like Margie, but
there are slight differences. This doll is unmarked,
while Margie was marked with a label on her
chest. There is a slight difference in the hair,
mouth, and the shape of the shoes. There is no
mention in any of the Cameo Doll Company files
that shows or mentions a 19" version. Another
company, Birnblick Toy Co. out of New York,
made a "knock off," or copy, of the Margie Doll.
Since Margie was such a popular doll at the time,
the Birnblick Toy Co. wanted to capitalize on it.
They named their doll Bette—and she looks almost exactly like Margie. She came in
various sizes including a 10" version. I believe the larger doll to be a Bette Doll and
not a Margie, but there will be others who will differ with me. Standing next to her
Raggedy Ann friend, Margie has painted features with opened mouth and teeth
showing, molded head, and wood-jointed body. Courtesy of Seaview Antique Dolls.

MICKEY MOUSE
Though unmarked, this appears to be a Cameo Doll with the same features as Pete the Pup and Bimbo. Wood-jointed arms and legs with two-piece composition body; painted, pie-eyed features; leather ears, red nose; 8 1/2", $1,000 and up, in original condition. Courtesy of Dan Sumpter.

Nearly identical to the other Mickey Mouse pictured, this model is 1" shorter at 7 1/2", with red feet and hooks put in the hand area. Leather ears, composition, wood-jointed, marked "1928." One of these in original condition sold at an auction in New England in 1997 for $2,800. Courtesy of Robert Greene.

TIMOTHY MOUSE
Possibly a Cameo Doll, this rare mouse is composition and wood, with painted features. There is a reference in a 1942 Playthings Magazine *ad to a Timothy Mouse who bears a striking resemblance to this piece that was being produced by the Cameo Doll Company. There were to be three Disney dolls manufactured, including Dumbo, Baby Weens, and Timothy Mouse. Dumbo was manufactured, but there is no evidence that Baby Weens nor Timothy Mouse were ever produced. The ad states that Dumbo was to be manufactured immediately while Timothy Q. Mouse and Baby Weens were to follow. To my knowledge, that never happened. The ad continues to state, "There are few manufacturers in the doll industry as well-known as Mr. Kallus. He has been producing dolls depicting well-known character and personality dolls for over 25 years, and has been credited with items whose sales have reached great volume. The Walt Disney items which Mr. Kallus will produce will be designed in his own inimitable way—of segmented wood and composition." It went on to say that new models would be available at Toy Fair, a buying show for retailers. Since this piece was found in the area of the Cameo Doll Company's factory, it could very well be a prototype. Courtesy of Robert Greene.*

MR. PEANUT—1935 *Composition and segment-ed wood with hat, stick, and flag; sold at the 1940 New York World's Fair, $175-$275 (Note: Only the World's Fair Mr. Peanut carried flag). Courtesy of Irene's Archives.*

PETE THE PUP—1932
Pete the Pup was originally planned to be a comic strip character; however, the plans to produce the comic strip fell through. Composition head, wood-segmented body came in various color combinations, sizes 9"-10", $150-$225; 12", $175-$275; 15", $250-$350.

Ad for Mr. Peanut celebrating his twentieth birthday in 1926. Courtesy of Nineteenth Century Imprints, Elisabeth Burdon.

Above are two sample comic strips that Joseph Kallus drew and planned to produce.

PINKIE—1930
Pinkie with green body and shoes; composition head, wood-jointed body—like Margie, only with a baby head—molded head, painted features, 9" & 10", $300-$400. Courtesy of Susan Ackerman.

PINOCCHIO—1940
Composition head, wood-segmented body; another doll manufactured by the Ideal Doll Co.; a Walt Disney-Joseph Kallus design, 7" & 8", $225-325; 11", $325-$450; 20", $375-$575. Author's Collection.

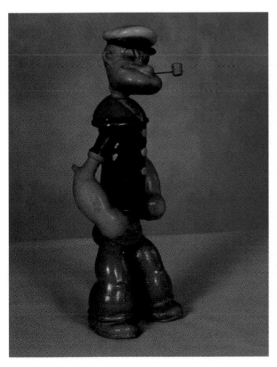

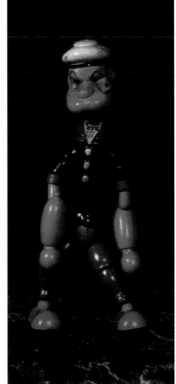

POPEYE—1935
Great 12 1/2" Popeye (left), all composition, jointed throughout arms and legs, great detail with decal, $350-$500. Courtesy of Sunnie Newell. Other Popeye versions included one with composition head and wood-segmented body, licensed by King Feature Syndicate, 14 1/2", $275-$550; 13 1/2" squeak toy, 1930s, $375.

A wonderful example of Popeye, 16", $450-$600. Courtesy of Irene's Archives.

RCA Radiotron—1930
Also called the "Selling Fool," composition head with a radio tube, wood-segmented body, slits in hands to hold business cards, 15 1/2", $1,000-$1,500. An advertising doll for the RCA Company. Irene's Archives.

Santa—1935
Composition figure made for the Shaeffer Pen Co. had hole in one hand to hold pen. 9 1/2", $250 and up. Courtesy of Jesco Corp.

THE FOLLOWING LIST INCLUDES THE DOLLS JOSEPH KALLUS DESIGNED THAT ARE NOT PICTURED

Baby Bundie—1918
All composition, 12", jointed arms, wig of mohair, painted features.
All composition, 16", fully jointed.

Bo-Fair—1919
Composition

Dollie—1921
Composition

Vanitie—1921
Composition

Baby Snooks (Fanny Brice)—1939
Composition head and hands, wooden feet, coiled wire body. Though a Joseph Kallus creation, this doll was manufactured by the Ideal Doll Co., 12", $200-$300. (See Chapter 7, "The Ideal Toy Corporation and The Shirley Temple Dolls.")

Bonzo (the dog)—1928
Composition. Sold exclusively to the carnival trade through a contract with Geo. Borgfeldft, 12"-14", $700 and up.

Champ—1942
Composition Boy Doll. It advertised "Now it's ok for your little boy to have a doll."

Jiminy Cricket—1940
Composition head, wood-segmented body, manufactured by the Ideal Doll Co., a Walt Disney design, 9", $500-$750.
(See Chapter 7, "The Ideal Toy Corporation and The Shirley Temple Dolls.")

Sissie—1928
All composition, jointed shoulders & hips to stand alone, painted hair, painted face, distributed by Butler Brothers.

Superman—Late 1940s
Composition head, wood-segmented body, 12 1/2"-13", $1,000 and up. Faster than a speeding bullet . . . Superman flew into our lives, first as a comic strip and then as a doll by the Ideal Doll Co.—and designed by Joseph Kallus (See Chapter 7, "The Ideal Toy Corporation and The Shirley Temple Dolls.")

OTHER DOLLS DESIGNED BY JOSEPH KALLUS IN THE 1940S, 1950S, AND 1960S THAT ARE VINYL

BABY—1940S
Vinyl head, magic skin arms & legs, cloth body, inset eyes, 17 1/2".

BABY MINE—1961
Vinyl, fully jointed, 18" & 20", $95-$150.

DYE-A-BABE—1956
Vinyl, fully jointed, drink & wet doll.

FELIX THE CAT—LATE 1950S
Vinyl, fully jointed.

HO-HO—1940
The little laughing Buddha, made in plaster, $35; made in vinyl in 1965; 3", $25; 5", $30-$35; 7", $35-$50.

MARGIE—1958
Vinyl, fully jointed, sleep eyes, rooted hair, 17", $110.

MISS PEEP—1957 & 1969
Vinyl, fully jointed, hinge joints, painted hair & eyes, 16"-18", $65-$90; 20", white or black, $110-$135. Add $50-$75 more for original box.

PINKIE—1950S
Vinyl, fully jointed, rooted hair, 27", $150-$175.

PEANUT—1958
Vinyl, fully jointed, drink & wet doll, 18 1/2".

POPEYE—1957-1959
Vinyl, fully jointed.

SCOOTLES—1964
Vinyl, 14", $150; up to 19", $250; up to 27", $350.

OTHER DOLLS MADE BY THE CAMEO DOLL COMPANY

BABY ADELE DOLLS—1930
Cameo Catalog photograph of Baby Adele. Composition head, hands, and legs; opened mouth; sleep eyes; $450 and up.

BYE-LO BABY DESIGNED BY GRACE PUTNAM
Composition head made by Cameo Doll Co., composition body made by Konig & Wericke, 1922, distributed by George Borgfeldt, New York, New York; 13" head circumference; $300-$450. Courtesy of Pat Wood.

Kewpies—1930s-1940s
All composition, 8", $150; 11"-12", $200-$250; 13", $250-$325; black doll 12"-13", $350-$400. Composition head with cloth body, 12", $225. Courtesy of Sunnie Newell.

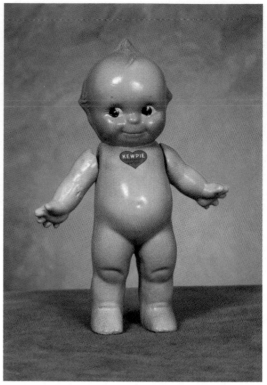

Composition Kewpie, 1913, with original label on chest.

Hard to find Black Kewpie, 12".

Left: Pencil sketch of Kewpidoodle Dog from Joseph Kallus's files. Courtesy of Jesco Corp.

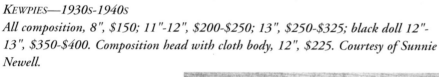

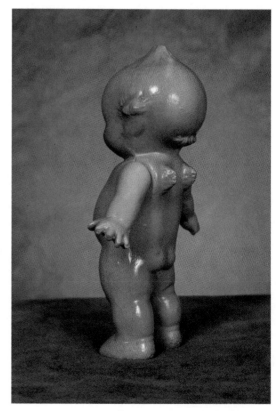

Shows back view with blue wings, 11 1/2", molded head, painted features, $250-$300. Author's Collection.

Original Cameo Doll Company photograph of Scootles mold.

SCOOTLES—1930-1935
The Scootles pictured above is all composition with painted features and molded hair; $450-$500. This 12" version from 1925 was designed by Rose O'Neill. Author's Collection. Other Scootles dolls were made in both black and white versions. They featured painted eyes looking forward or to the side, and a few have sleep eyes. Black version, 12", $600-$800; white version, 7 1/2", $325-$425; 10", $375-$450; 12", $450-$525; 13", $450-$525; 15", $550-$650; 16", $550-$650; 20", $700-$900.

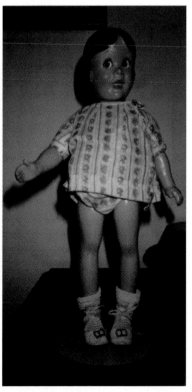

LITTLE ANNIE ROONEY
There were two Little Annie Rooney Dolls produced. One was made after the character in the cartoon strip by Jack Collins—the other was an interpretation of Mary Pickford from her role in the movie Little Annie Rooney.

The doll pictured here was from the cartoon strip by Jack Collins. Composition molded head with painted features, side glancing eyes, black painted hair, composition body, made in 1925, redressed. In all original condition, $550-$700. Courtesy of Susan Ackerman.

Above: Advertisement for Little Annie Rooney Doll. Shown in Playthings, *January 1926.*

All original Scootles, 16", $550-$650. Courtesy of Pat Wood.

Jerry Mahoney, all original, $450 and up. Courtesy of Pat Wood.

CHAPTER TWO
CHARACTER DOLLS & TOYS

The fun of character collectibles is abounding in this book. There has got to be a character in everyone's past that they fondly remember, whether it be Betty Boop and her dog, Bimbo; Popeye; or a real life character like Charlie Chaplin. The characters you will see cross over the line of age and become a welcome sight for young and old. I certainly was not around when Betty Boop was having her heyday in the comic strips, but that doesn't stop me from enjoying her now. Character dolls and toys tend to keep their value very well—and continue to put smiles on collectors' faces.

Excellent example of Jerry Mahoney with his original box, $500 and up. Courtesy of Frank's Toys.

Alexander, Dagwood's son from the popular comic strip "Blondie," all composition with painted features, molded head, 9 1/2", made by Knickerbocker Doll & Toy Company, $450 and up. Courtesy of Carl Kludt.

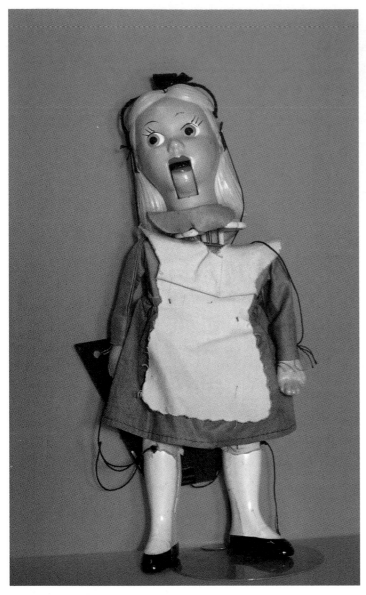

A composition and wood-jointed Betty Boop with oversized head; wearing a short red dress; 12 1/2", $750-$1,000. Courtesy of Christie's Images.

Alice in Wonderland Puppet, made by Peter Puppet Playthings, 14", $125-$150. Courtesy of Gasoline Alley.

Right: Two sizes of Bonzo, wood-jointed tail with composition body, molded head, painted features. Smaller version shows original label on chest. Small, $600 and up; larger version, $1,000 and up. Courtesy of Annette's Antique Dolls.

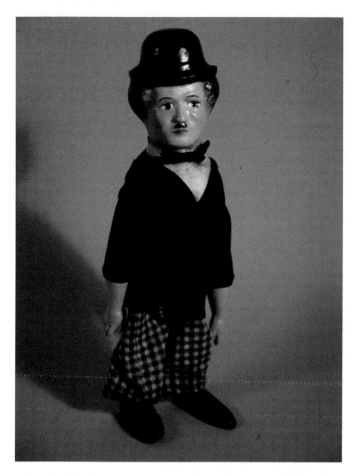

Charlie Chaplin, composition and metal wind-up doll, 12",
$400 and up. Courtesy of Carl Kludt.

Charlie McCarthy Hand Puppet. Excellent condition,
composition head with cloth, $150. Courtesy of
Gasoline Alley.

Curly Kayoe. All composition, 12 1/2", $200-$250.
Courtesy of Carl Kludt.

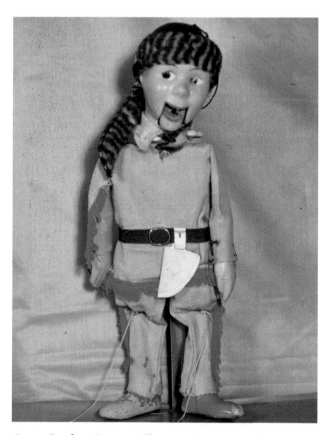

Davy Crockett Puppet. All original, nice example, $150.
Courtesy of Gasoline Alley.

Dick Tracy, all composition, 13 1/2", mouth opens and closes, $200-$250. Courtesy of Carl Kludt.

Ferdinand the Bull Hand Puppet. Composition head with cloth, $125-$150. Courtesy of Gasoline Alley.

Denny Dimwit Doll. "He Wiggles, He Waggles, He's Smart, He's Friendly," made in 1948, composition with molded features, red molded hat, green painted gloves, brown shoes, painted features, swings and sways back and forth, $250-$375.

Dog, composition molded head, cloth body, 17", possibly Buster Brown's dog, $275-$350. Courtesy of Sunnie Newell.

Grouping of Felix the Cats. Large, green Felix is all composition with molded features, decal on chest and tail of wired mesh, $1,000 and up. Pink Felix is described as green Felix with arms that reach out. The pink is the rarest of the Felix Dolls, priced at $1,200 and up. Below, two oriental style Felix the Cats in red and black, wood-jointed with composition heads (notice slits for eyes), leather ears; red, $400-$500; black, $300-$400. Courtesy of Collector's Paradise.

Close-up of oriental Felix the Cat, with original chest label, flexible arms and legs with wooden hands, feet, and tail. Rare, olive coloring, 3 1/2", $450-$550. Courtesy of Dan Sumpter.

This push-up Felix the Cat was made in 1995; it retails for around $6; a nice copy of an old favorite. Courtesy of Dan Sumpter.

Howdy Doody with composition head, hands, cloth legs, and body in original outfit with scarf marked "Howdy Doody," $350-$450.

Herby, 12", all composition, $200-$250. Courtesy of Carl Kludt.

Left: An unusual papier-mache and cloth "Jiggs" nodder; glass eyes, black suit, spats, cigar, cane; originally a store display. Jiggs is a character from the comic strip "Bringing Up Father"; 21", $3,000 and up. Courtesy of Christie's Images.

Above: Composition Krazy Kat, black body with red molded hands, painted features, free standing, $175-$275. Courtesy of Aurora Antique Mall. (Alhough I believe this to be a copy of Krazy Kat, there was a Warner Brothers' character made in 1931 named "Foxy"— which is very similar.)

Above: Little Orphan Annie with cup, 14"; doll made by Freund-lich Novelty Corp; $275-$350. Courtesy of Carl Kludt.

Little Orphan Annie, all original, showing molding of head. Author's Collection.

Lucky Lindy Doll, composition with molded head, great smile, painted hair and features, cloth body, original aviator's outfit, $750. Courtesy of Rosalie Whyel Museum of Doll Art.

A pair of May & Moritz Walkers, both 7 1/2", wood and composition figures dressed in period clothing with a black and white wooden pig and wheelbarrow, $600 and up. Courtesy of Christie's Images.

Character Puppet of the Mad Hatter, 14 1/2", composition hands, feet, and head with cloth body, $125-$150. Courtesy of Gasoline Alley.

Right: Peter Pan Marionette, cloth body with composition head, hands, and feet; unmarked, mouth opens and closes, molded hair, painted features, original green outfit with brown molded and painted boots, $100-$125.

Far Right: Peter Pan Character Marionette, cloth body with composition head, hands, and feet; unmarked, mouth opens and closes, molded hair, painted features, original blue dress with painted yellow shoes, $75-$100.

Policeman, 6", all wood, jointed at arms—flip his lever and watch him flip his hat! (Below) Painted features, blue hat and uniform, metal lever in back, $110-$150.

Close-up of Popeye by Chein, 8 1/2", with original Sea Bag, $700 and up. Courtesy of Dan Sumpter.

Left: Souvenir, World's Fair Popeye, 1933, 8 1/4", recently sold at auction for $1,600. Courtesy of Keystone Toy Trader.

Punch and Judy Theater, characters have composition heads, with cloth bodies; nice early pieces; $650 and up. Courtesy of Cobb's Doll Auction.

Punch and Judy Puppets with friends, early 1900s, composition heads with cloth bodies and wooden hands—a nice collection of these early puppets, $250 (each) and up. Courtesy of James & Judy Sneed.

Left: Close-up of Punch & Judy Puppets. Courtesy of James & Judy Sneed.

Grace Drayton's "Puppy Pippin" with friends, stuffed cloth body with composition head, painted eyes and molded ears, $250-$400. Courtesy of Cobb's Doll Auctions.

Toby, comic character from comic strip, marked "C 1932 Toby," all composition, molded head, painted features, 10", $300 and up. Author's Collection.

Tonto and the Lone Ranger, two great dolls in excellent condition. The Lone Ranger stands 16", all composition, $350-$375. Tonto is 16" and all composition, $350-$375. Courtesy of Annette's Antique Dolls.

Lone Ranger. Courtesy of Carl Kludt.

An unusual painted composition figure of Mama Katzenjammer pulling Hans and Fritz apart, 6 1/4", $300-$500. Courtesy of Christie's Images.

Miss Curity, advertising doll, molded composition with painted features, ca. 1950, $150-$275.

A wooden, jointed, and cloth figure of Spark Plug from the "Barney Google" comic strip. Spark Plug wears a vivid yellow, patched horse blanket; 9", $350-$500. Courtesy of Christie's Images.

Left: A Syrocco Composition figure of Superman, in a wood finish, standing in full costume, 6", $800-$1,200. Courtesy of Christie's Images.

Sad Sack, all original with composition molded head, composition hands and cloth body, original brown uniform with black tie and brown belt, painted features, $400-$500. Courtesy of Annette's Antique Dolls.

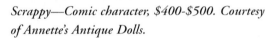

Scrappy—Comic character, $400-$500. Courtesy of Annette's Antique Dolls.

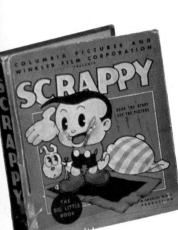

Book of Scrappy— Comic character.

Right: Hand Puppet—Jimmy Durante's Umbriago. Composition head with cloth, made by American Merchandise Distributors, 1945, $100-$150. Courtesy of Gasoline Alley.

Marionette of Tramp from Disney's Lady and the Tramp, composition with jointed legs, painted features, fabric ears, $75-$100. Courtesy of Annette's Antique Dolls.

Wood-jointed Donald Duck, 16", with painted features and long bill. He is wearing a blue sailor suit, and a hat with a red bow; unauthorized and unmarked, $500-$750. Author's Collection.

CHAPTER THREE
DISNEY DOLLS & TOYS

I n the Golden Age of Disney, ca. 1930s, you will see that a large variety of wood and composition dolls and toys were available. Through the master of merchandising, a huge selection of items can be had by the beginning collector, as well as the more advanced.

When Mickey Mouse first appeared in *Steamboat Willie* in 1928, few would know the tremendous response that this little mouse would have on the world. Many characters would follow, including Donald Duck, Minnie Mouse, Pluto, and Pinocchio, to name a few. From wooden crib toys to complete sets like Snow White and the Seven Dwarfs, the different items you could buy seemed endless. For this reason, the selection of older Disney items, though not plentiful, are more readily available than many of the other collectibles in this book.

With the reissues of such favorites as *Snow White and the Seven Dwarfs* and *Pinocchio* on video tape, a new generation of collectors can see the characters so many of us enjoyed as children. These collectors and others will be looking for pieces that came with the original movies, making those items increasingly valuable.

Disney will, I'm sure, continue to work its magic and bring us a wonderful new array of characters and related products to collect.

All Disney authorized pieces shown in this book are copyrighted by Walt Disney Productions or Walt Disney Enterprises.

Below, and on page 42, is a collection of unauthorized (not approved by Disney) pieces including Donald Duck, Pluto, and Mickey Mouse. They were made in Sweden, probably in the late 1950s, and manufactured by Gemla. I purchased these toys from Treasure Valley Antiques in Nampa, Idaho.

Unauthorized wood-jointed Mickey Mouse, 10", with painted features, red pants, yellow shirt, and black and white limbs; marked "Sweden" on foot, $500-$750. Author's Collection.

Bambi, made with a very unusual oversized composition molded head; opened mouth, painted eyes; jointed legs with three-piece body; $750 and up. Possibly a prototype by Joseph Kallus. Courtesy of Susan Ackerman.

Unauthorized, wood-jointed Pluto, 8", with painted features in yellow and red, marked "Sweden" on foot, $350-$500. Author's Collection.

Group shot from front with Donald, Mickey Mouse, and Pluto. Author's Collection.

Group shot with rear view of Donald and Mickey Mouse. Author's Collection.

DISNEY MARIONETTES

Composition and strings, 10"-12", $100-$350, depending on piece and character.

Donald Duck Puppet, $125-$150. Courtesy of
Gasoline Alley.

*A different Donald Duck Puppet with red vest;
very cute, nice example, $150. Courtesy of
Gasoline Alley.*

*Close-up of rare Donald Duck, Fun-E-Flex, origi-
nally came with sleigh, 3", $800-$1,000. Courtesy
of Gasoline Alley.*

*Wonderful Donald Duck Puppet,
with a combination of composition and wood, $125-$150.
Courtesy of Gasoline Alley.*

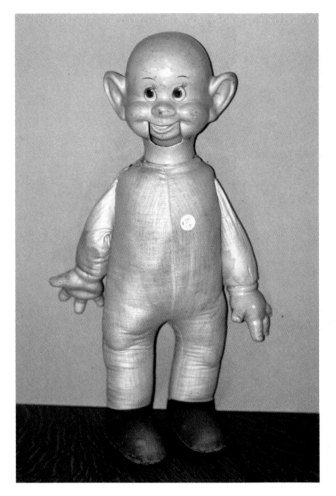

Dopey Hand Puppet. Composition head with cloth; painted features; $125-$150. Author's Collection.

Dopey Ventriloquist Doll, very rare, $350-$400; in original outfit, $500-$600. Author's Collection.

A different version of Dumbo with a composition head and large, molded ears; painted features, wood-jointed trunk, arms, and legs; composition molded red and green body. Marked "DUMBO" on bow tie; rare piece, possibly a prototype of a Joseph Kallus doll; $500 and up. Courtesy of Susan Ackerman.

Grumpy from the Seven Dwarfs; composition, jointed at shoulders, painted features, mohair wig or beard, velvet outfit with cap. Sneezy, Dopey, Grumpy, Doc, Happy, Sleepy, and Bashful were the names of the Seven Dwarfs, and the names appeared across the top of their caps; 9" tall, $250-$275 each. Author's Collection.

Two of the Knickerbocker Seven Dwarfs, one undressed to show the one-piece body, all original, $225-$275. Author's Collection.

Figaro, who played the cat in Pinocchio, all composition, jointed at the legs, 7", hard item to find, $400 and up. Author's Collection.

The three are at it again! Here is an Ideal Pinocchio with Jiminy Cricket and Figaro. (See description in Chapter 7, "The Ideal Toy Corporation & The Shirley Temple Dolls") Author's Collection.

A great example of a large Fun-E-Flex Mickey Mouse, 1931-1932, 9", marked "Mickey Mouse Des Patent 82802 by Walt Disney," $1,500-$2,000 and up. Courtesy of Gasoline Alley.

Fun-E-Flex Minnie Mouse, all original, good condition, 4", $175-$250. Courtesy of Gasoline Alley.

The Pelham Puppets Display, featuring the Disney characters, is located in Chapter 14.

Donald, Pelham Puppet, $125-$150. Courtesy of Gasoline Alley.

Multicolored Mickey Mouse, marked "West Germany," 1950s, colorful body in wood segments, movable arms with wooden hands, wooden feet with orange and green shoes, hand-painted features, 10", $175-$275. Courtesy of Dan Sumpter.

Fun-E-Flex Minnie Mouse, $550. Courtesy of Gasoline Alley.

Early 1920s, rare 4 1/2" Micky, all wood with wire type tail, marked "Borgfelt" on label on foot, $350 and up. Courtesy of Gasoline Alley.

This photo shows the comparison of the Minnie and Mickey Mouse Fun-E-Flex Toys, each 3 1/2", marked "Walt E. Disney," identical, except for white spots on Minnie's dress and black spots on Mickey, $175-$275. Courtesy of Dan Sumpter.

Fun-E-Flex Mickey Mouse, great example, 3 1/2", 1930s, label on chest. Courtesy of Vicki E. Barnes.

Paco from Walt Disney's The Three Caballeros.
*Composition head and body with wooden hat,
hands, and feet. Yellow and green with orange
feet and orange, molded beak; lighter orange hat,
painted eyes. Rare piece, $500 and up. Courtesy
of Susan Ackerman.*

*Panchito the Chicken, 1941, a Walt Disney character. A very rare and unusual piece.
Composition molded head with painted features and inset eyes, wood-jointed arms
and legs, composition body, $750 and up. Courtesy of Norma Carroll.*

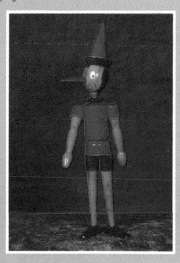

Pinocchio, unmarked, 16", very unusual, wood and composition, molded head, painted features. Believed to have been manufactured after the book by Collier entitled Pinocchio. This doll looks identical to the figure in the book; $275 and up. Courtesy of Sunnie Newell.

Pinocchio, unmarked, all wood-jointed at legs, shoulders, and head, 18" (came in a variety of sizes, 6"-4'), $75-$100.

Above: Pinocchio by Crown Toy Co., $275-$350. Author's Collection.

Pinocchio Hand Puppet, composition head with cloth body, $90-$150. Author's Collection.

Snow White and the Seven Dwarfs by Knickerbocker. Snow White is 15", marked "Walt Disney" on back of head, "Knickerbocker Toy Co., New York" on back, "Snow White by Walt Disney" on paper tag, "Knickerbocker Toy Co., Stuffed Animals, 650 Sixth Ave., New York, No.3, Snow White Doll" on box's end label. She is composition with hazel sleep eyes with real lashes, all original. The Seven Dwarfs are all 9", marked "©Walt Disney, Knickerbocker Toy Co." on backs, "Knickerbocker Toy Co. Stuffed Animals, 650 Sixth Ave., New York City," plus stock no. and name of dwarf stamped on box's end label. Beautiful set, $2,000-$3,000. Courtesy of McMaster's Doll Auction.

Seven Dwarf Dolls, cloth bodies with hard plastic faces, painted features, stapled-on ears, $275-$400. Courtesy of Gasoline Alley.

Knickerbocker Snow White with the Seven Dwarfs design on skirt. All composition, jointed at neck, shoulders, and hips. Black wig, sleep eyes, opened mouth, 16", $400-$500. Courtesy of Pat Wood.

Pop-up Pluto by Fisher Price. Wood-jointed toy on stand, $75-$100. Courtesy of Sunnie Newell.

Fun-E-Flex Pluto with longer yellow felt ears, larger piece on end of tail, distributed by George Borgfeldt Corp., 1930s, 4" long with tail, marked "PLUTO THE PUP," Walt Disney Enterprises, $300-$325. Courtesy of Vicki E. Barnes.

Fun-E-Flex Penguin, 3 1/2", marked "a Fun-E-Flex Toy," opened mouth-beak, painted eyes, fin arms, $75-$125. Many of the Fun-E-flex Toys are Disney related; this one is not. Courtesy of Dan Sumpter.

The Three Pigs, Fun-E-Flex, all original with original label on chests, $350-$500 for set. Courtesy of Marci.

Fun-E-Flex Pig from The Three Pigs, all wood with tail, pipe in mouth, arms that bend, chest label, 1930s, $150-$175. Courtesy of Dan Sumpter.

Tramp, from Disney's Lady and the Tramp, is featured on page 39, in Chapter 2.

CHAPTER FOUR
BLACK COMPOSITION DOLLS

As Susy and her father were walking past a store window, she stopped to gaze at the beautiful black baby doll that was in the window. It looked so pretty in its pink dress with ruffles! Dad, though, had little money for food, much less a new doll. But, when he saw the look on his little girl's face, he vowed to buy her that doll. With weeks of working extra hours and putting away whatever extra money he could scrape together, Susy's dream would come true.

Three months later, at Christmastime, as Susy unwrapped the large box that lay under the sparsely decorated tree, she had no idea that inside was the precious little baby doll she had dreamed and longed for. The happiness that child felt when she looked in that box was indescribable.

Today, children walk down the aisle of their favorite store and see rows of dolls and toys for the picking. Even the parent with the most modest means can usually manage to give that child at least one doll or toy. In the 1920s and 1930s, however, that was not the case. While there were, of course, the wealthy who could buy anything they wanted, the majority of the population was struggling to survive. With this in mind, you can imagine the amount of love and care that went into composition dolls and toys in the early days. Children knew that if something happened to their prized possession, it would not be easily replaced.

Black dolls, though not as plentiful as white dolls, can be found in every area of doll collecting, including bisque, composition, cloth, and hard plastic. But, the variety of composition black dolls, unfortunately, is limited. With the wear and tear that composition takes over the years with humidity, dust, sunlight, et cetera, it is difficult to find composition dolls in excellent condition. With the limited numbers of black dolls produced, and with Mother Nature playing its forces on these precious babies, finding a good selection to add to your collection can be a challenge.

Many people collect black dolls, and dolls in general, including talk show host Oprah Winfrey and movie star Demi Moore. Bisque dolls can run into the thousands of dollars, but many of the composition dolls available can be had for $100-$500, still making them affordable for most people, and a good investment for the future. Though called "black dolls," their colors can range from light brown to black. Included in this chapter are a wide variety of black composition dolls for your enjoyment.

Beautiful Black Doll with Mollye Goldman clothing and original Molly-`es tag; 10", $250 and up. Courtesy of Pat Wood.

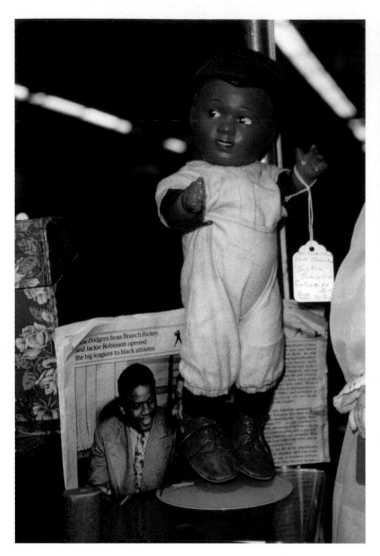

Jackie Robinson Doll, 13 1/2", composition with painted features, molded head, original clothing with baseball cap, $650 and up. Courtesy of Annette's Antique Dolls.

Tony Sarg's Mammy Doll, Marks: "Tony Sarg's Mammy Doll, Sole Distributors, Geo. Borgfeldt Corp. New York, NY" on gold paper label and on box's end label. Brown composition character head, painted brown eyes with heavily molded eyelids, single stroke brows, opened-closed smiling mouth with six painted teeth, original mohair wig, large gold hoop earrings, cloth body jointed at shoulders only, large composition hands and feet with molded and painted shoes. Dressed in original red and white print dress, white stockings. Mammy comes with 7 1/2" unmarked composition white baby, painted brown eyes to side, painted lashes, closed mouth, molded and painted brown hair, jointed at shoulders and hips. Baby is wearing knit undershirt, flannel diaper, socks tied with pink ribbons, and is wrapped in white flannel blanket tied with pink ribbon—a rare doll with its original box—$800-$1,200. Courtesy of McMaster's Doll Auctions.

Left: Unmarked Black Composition Baby, 10", jointed at shoulders and hips, $75. Courtesy of Lisa Sheets.

Googly-Eyed Dolls. On the left is a doll, 19", with sewn-on clothing. Black dolls, $150-$250; white dolls, $75-$150. They were marketed through Sears in 1948. Sunnie Newell Collection (See Chapter 13, "Unmarked Dolls," for more information.).

Black Googly-Eyed Doll, 21", with sewn-on clothing, $150-$250. Courtesy of Lynnae Ramsey.

Grouping of unmarked Black Baby Dolls; 8", 8 1/2", and 9"; all composition with molded hair, jointed at arms and legs, painted features, $85-$150. Courtesy of Lynnae Ramsey.

Unmarked Black Boy Doll, 12" with composition head and arms, cloth body, painted head and features, $150-$200.

This Googly has molded hair, all-fabric body, and composition head; 19", $150-$250. Courtesy of Sunnie Newell.

Right: Cynthia by Madame Alexander, the "Comb & Curl" doll with styling box; 14", composition with sleep eyes, painted mouth; jointed at arms and legs; all original; $700-$800. Courtesy of Pat Wood.

Below: Black Boy Doll, 16", all composition with painted eyes to side, molded hair and closed mouth, curved legs and arms, $150-$275. Courtesy of Lynnae Ramsey.

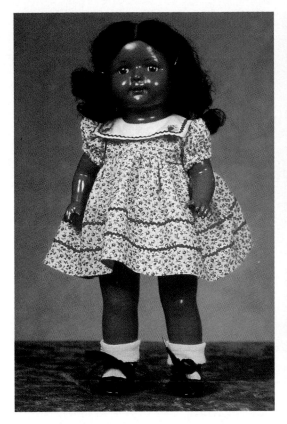

Black Effanbee Rosemary, 17", $400-$500.
Courtesy of Lynnae Ramsey.

Patsy Look-alike, composition with molded hair,
jointed at arms and legs, painted features, 17",
$250-$300. Courtesy of Lynnae Ramsey.

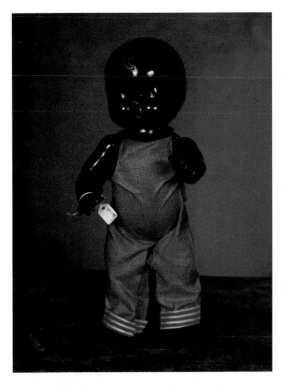

Puggy, "A Petite Doll" by American Character,
12", made in 1928, composition with molded
hair and painted features, $550 and up.
Courtesy of Pat Wood.

Topsy Black, 9", composition with painted features, molded hair to
hold ribbons, jointed at arms and legs, $85-$125. Courtesy of
Sunnie Newell.

Black Shirley Look-alike, with sleep eyes, mohair wig, $300-$400. Author's Collection.

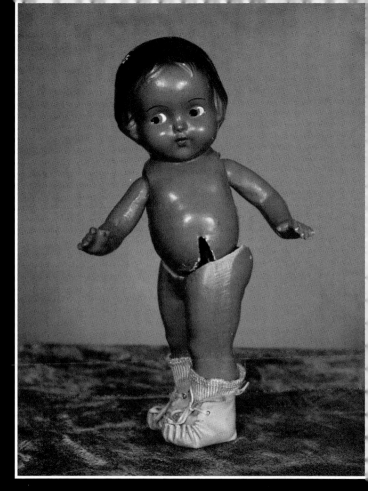

Black Composition Baby, 10", with twist body, "Patsy-type" molded hair with straight legs. $150. Courtesy of Pat Wood.

Same doll as left. Notice twist-and-turn body.

Mama Doll, 23", cloth body with composition arms, legs, and head; tin sleep eyes, $175-$225. A nice, early example. Susan Killoran Collection.

CHAPTER FIVE
THE EFFANBEE DOLL COMPANY &
THE PATSY FAMILY

The Effanbee Doll Company was founded by Bernard E. Fleishanker and Hugo Baum in 1910 as a toy and novelty company, with its main focus on manufacturing and distributing dolls. They ran the company from 1910 to 1940, when it was sold after the death of Hugo Baum. The "Eff" stood for Bernard E. Fleishanker, and the "bee" stood for Hugo Baum.

Based in New York, in the 1920s, they built the Effanbee Doll Company into one of the largest doll companies in the United States.

In the 1930s, the Patsy Doll Club was very popular, with over 275,000 members. Effanbee's "Aunt Patsy" promoted the Patsy line of dolls by traveling around the country, making public appearances. She kept little admirers of the Patsy Dolls informed through a publication called the *Patsytown News*, the club's own newspaper, plus another publication called *My Doll's Magazine*.

In 1946, the company was sold to Noma Electric, a company that manufactured Christmas tree lights. During the time that Noma Electric ran the company, it fell to a lower position in the doll industry. Being a company that specialized in Christmas lights rather than dolls, the firm just didn't give the dolls—nor the Effanbee Company—the attention they deserved. In 1953, the family of Bernard E. Fleishanker bought back the company and tried to return it to its higher standard of quality in the doll community.

After the Fleishanker family helped to restore the company to what they felt was a satisfactory level, they sold it again in 1971. This time, however, it was sold to someone who cared about dolls—someone who had experience in the doll and toy industry. Roy R. Raizen and Leroy Fadem became the proud new owners of the Effanbee Doll Company—but this was not to be a long-lasting relationship. They sold out in 1987, and then the doll maker was sold again in 1992 to the Alexander Doll Group. Stanley and Irene Wahberg took control and began to build the Effanbee Doll Company into a leader in the doll industry. They took the most popular doll that Effanbee had made, the Patsy Joan Doll, and reproduced it in every detail. This gave new collectors an opportunity to own what their grandmothers before them had owned. The new Patsy Joan was released through the JC Penney and FAO Schwarz catalogs. With nearly 90 years in the doll business, and after many changes in ownership, the Effanbee Doll company is here to stay.

Ad for Effanbee Dolls. Courtesy of Nineteenth Century Imprints, Elisabeth Burdon.

AMISH COUPLE

12" Amish Grumpy Man and Woman, marked "Effanbee Dolls, Walk, Talk, Sleep" on back of shoulder plate; "Pennsylvania Dutch Dolls, by Marie Polack, Reg. U.S. Pat. Off." on one side of small paper tag, "Amish" on the other side of tag. Composition shoulder heads, painted blue eyes to side, closed pouty mouth, original mohair wigs, mohair beard on man, cloth body with composition arms and feet with molded and painted shoes on man, composition legs on woman. Woman is dressed in original white panties, brown flannel slip, blue cotton dress, black apron and shawl, white organdy bonnet under black outer bonnet, socks, and shoes. Man is dressed in original denim pants and jacket, green knit piece on front under jacket to look like shirt, black felt hat; $300-$400 for pair. Courtesy of McMaster's Doll Auctions.

American Child, 20", marked "Effanbee Anne-Shirley" on back; "I am an Effanbee Durable Doll, the Doll with the Satin-Smooth Skin" on paper wrist tag; "Effanbee Durable Dolls, Made in USA" on tag on back of dress. Metal heart bracelet, composition head, green sleep eyes, real lashes, opened mouth with four upper teeth, original human hair wig, five-piece composition body with large hands, dressed in original teal blue dress, pink eyelet-trimmed pinafore, one-piece underwear combination, blue straw hat, $1,000 and up. Courtesy of McMaster's Doll Auctions.

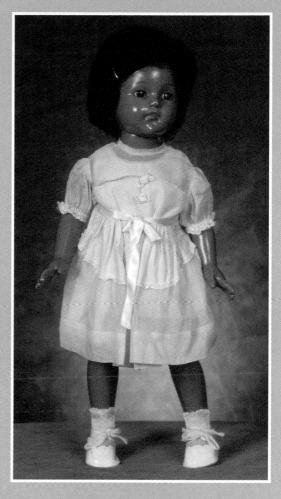

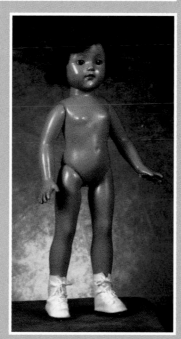

*Black Anne Shirley, all composition, sleep eyes, 21",
1935-1940, $500-$650. Author's Collection.*

*Top Left: All original, 24" Anne Shirley, $425-
$500. Courtesy of Pat Wood.*

*ANNE SHIRLEY—1935-1940
Composition, sleep eyes, closed mouth, eye-
lashes, same face as Little Lady (During the
war, some dolls were made with yarn hair
and painted features.), 13"-14", $225-
$275; 17"-18", $275-$325; 21", $375-
$425; 24", $425-$500; 27", $475-$575.*

*Anne Shirley, 21", five-piece
composition body, sleep eyes,
mohair wig. Courtesy of
Susan Killoran.*

*Left: Anne Shirley, 18", yarn
hair, redressed (if original
clothing, $275-$325). Courtesy
of Sunnie Newell.*

BABY GRUMPY—1912
Composition with painted features, 11", $250-$300. Author's Collection.

BRIGHT EYES—1946
Composition with flirty eyes, wig, 22", $350. Courtesy of Lynnae Ramsey.

BUBBLES—1924

Composition head, legs, curved arms; cloth body; opened mouth, molded hair, sleep eyes; 16", $225; 18", $295; 20", $300; 22", $325-$350; 25", $400-$475. Original retail prices range from about $3 to $5. Author's Collection.

Bubbles, 22", $350-$400 (notice original bracelet). Courtesy of Pat Wood.

Right: Bubbles, 25", $400-$475. Courtesy of Lynnae Ramsey.

CHARLIE MCCARTHY—1937

Composition head, feet, and hands; painted eyes and painted hair, marked "Edgar Bergen's Charlie McCarthy, an Effanbee Product," 17"-20", $475-$525, Mint-In-Box, $675.

Charlie McCarthy, 20"; marks: "Edgar Bergen's Charlie McCarthy, an Effanbee Product" on back of shoulder plate. Composition shoulder head, painted brown eyes with red liner, multi-stroke brows, opened mouth with ten lower teeth painted on lower jaw; pink cloth body with composition hands and feet; stitch-jointed at shoulders, hips, and knees. Dressed in original tuxedo, white shirt, tie, vest, black pants, and jacket with tails and top hat. Courtesy of McMaster's Doll Auctions.

Above & Left: All original Charlie McCarthy. Made in 1939, Ventriloquist Doll. Courtesy of Pat Wood.

Ad with Charlie McCarthy and Edgar Bergen for GE Lamps. Courtesy of Nineteenth Century Prints, Elisabeth Burdon.

HISTORICAL SERIES
Made in 1939, composition, jointed at arms and legs. Portrayed the history of American fashion from 1492-1939. "American Children" heads with painted eyes and human hair wigs, came with metal heart bracelet, marked on body "EFFanBEE ANNE SHIRLEY."

Above Left: Two additional Effanbee Historical Replica Dolls. At right is the 1750-The Development of Culture Doll, with composition head, painted blue eyes, dark brown beauty mark on right cheek, original white mohair wig, and five-piece composition body, with large hands. She is dressed in an original blue quilted skirt, with blue floral overdress lined with red, and has original underclothing, long stockings, and shoes; $400-$600.

At left is the 1868-Postwar Period Doll, with composition head, painted brown eyes, closed mouth, human hair wig, and five-peice composition body. She is dressed in original red-white checked dress with white apron, original underclothing, long stockings, and shoes; $400-$600. Courtesy of McMaster's Doll Auctions.

Above Right: Two Effanbee Historical Replica Dolls. At left is the 1872-Economic Development Doll marked "Effanbee, Anne-Shirley" on back, and "Effanbee Durable Doll" on her bracelet. Composition head, painted blue eyes, closed mouth, original human hair wig in original set, five-piece composition body; dressed in original, rust-colored, long gown with tiered skirt with removable bustle. $400-$600.

At right is the 1939-Today Doll. Composition head, painted blue eyes, closed mouh, human hair wig, five-piece composition body. Dressed in a white lace top, pink skirt, and green sash (sold for $460 at McMaster's Doll Auctions). Courtesy of McMaster's Doll Auctions.

Left: Two more Effanbee Historical Replica Dolls. At left is the 1492-Primitive Indian Doll, with reddish brown composition head, painted brown eyes, painted upper and lower lashes, closed mouth, original human hair wig, and five-piece composition body with large hands. Dressed in original gray leather Indian outfit, with no underclothing, socks, or shoes, $400-$700 (sold at McMaster's Doll Auctions for $750).

At right is the 1896-Unity of Nation Established Doll, with composition head, painted brown eyes, painted upper and lower lashes, closed mouth, original human hair wig, and five-piece composition body, with large hands. Dressed in original coral outfit, with white blouse with jabot and full sleeves, underclothing, long stockings, and shoes. $400-$500. Courtesy of McMaster's Doll Auctions.

LITTLE LADY—1940-1949
All original Little Lady with wig and original paper tag and box.
Composition, mohair wig or yard type hair, 17"-18". Doll only,
$300-$400; with box, add $75. Courtesy of Pat Wood.

LITTLE GIRL
Little Girl, 9", $160, Sunnie Newell Collection.

LOVUMS
1928 Marked "EffanBee Lovums COPYR 1924,"
composition with wig or painted hair, sleep eyes,
opened smiling mouth, 16"-18", $250-$325;
22"-24", $350-$425; 28" (right), $500.
Courtesy of Lannae Ramsey.

Close-up of handle to wind the record for the Mae Starr Doll.

MAE STARR
Two beautiful examples of the Mae Starr Doll. All composition with cloth body that held a record player; 25", $600 and up. Courtesy of Lynnae Ramsey.

Close-up of record mechanism for Mae Starr Doll.

All original Mae Starr. Courtesy of Pat Wood.

MICKEY 1939-1949
Composition with sleep eyes; molded, painted hair; closed mouth;
16"-18", $275-$325; 22"-24", $325-$400.
Courtesy of Lannae Ramsey.

MARY LEE
Marked "Mary Lee by EFFanBEE," all original, 19", sleep eyes
with composition arms, legs, and head; cloth body, human hair
wig. Mary Lee in this condition with box, $450 and up. Courtesy
of Pat Wood.

PATRICIA
Composition, human hair wig,
sleep eyes, sometimes molded
and painted hair, 15". Pictured
to the right is an Effanbee
Patricia, all original with red
hair, $400-$450. Courtesy of
Pat Wood.

A wonderful grouping of the Patsy Family. Sunnie Newell Collection.

PATSY

Composition with sleep or painted eyes, molded hair; original felt hat and coat; 14", $350 and up.

Sleep-eyed Patsy on left, Painted-eye Patsy on right, all original. Courtesy of Pat Wood.

Patsy in green dress, 13". Sunnie Newell Collection.

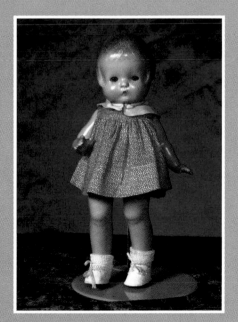

Patsy in red dress, 13". Sunnie Newell Collection.

New reproductions of the dolls: (left) the Patsy in red from JC Penney; the Patsy in the blue outfit was issued through FAO Schwartz; $75-$100 each. Courtesy of Sunnie Newell.

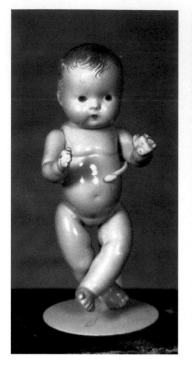

BABY OR PATSY TINYETTE—1927
Composition, molded and paint-
ed hair, painted eyes, 7", $200-
$250.

Above Baby Tinyette, 7", $225-
$250. Courtesy of Sunnie
Newell.

Patsy Baby, $275-$350, dressed in original cloth-
ing. Courtesy of Lynnae Ramsey.

PATSY JR.
Composition, molded and painted hair,
painted eyes, 11", $300-$350. Courtesy of
Sunnie Newell.

PATSY ANN
Composition, wig or molded and painted hair,
sleep eyes, inset lashes, 19", $450-$500. Sunnie
Newell Collection.

PATSYETTE
Composition, molded hair, 9", $300-$350.
Courtesy of Lynnae Ramsey.

PATSY BABYETTE
Composition, wig or molded and painted hair, painted eyes, 8", $250-$275. Courtesy of Sunnie Newell.

PATSY JOAN
Composition, wig or molded and painted hair, sleep eyes, inset lashes, 16", $500-$600. Courtesy of Sunnie Newell.

PATSY LOU
Composition, wig or molded and painted hair, sleep eyes, inset lashes, 22", $500-$550. Courtesy of Sunnie Newell.

Above: All original Patsy Lou, $500-$600. Courtesy of Pat Wood.

BARBARA ANN
Composition, 17", $575-$650.

BARBARA JOAN
Composition, 15", $450-$475.

BARBARA LOU
Composition, 21", $650-$700.

BETTY BRITE—1933
Composition, 16 1/2", $275-$300.

BLACK PATSY
Composition, molded hair, three tufts of braided hair,
14", $500.

GLORIA ANN
Composition, closed mouth, sleep eyes, 20", $850-$900.

HEART BEAT BABY—1948
Composition with cloth body, sleep eyes, hair lashes, has
key-wound mechanism in body; 20", $175.

HONEY—1948-49
Composition, human hair wig, 21", $375.

MARILEE—1924
Composition with cloth body; mohair wig, sleep eyes,
opened mouth with upper teeth, 24", $275.

PATRICIA KIN
Composition, molded hair, 11", $225.

PATSY MAE
Composition, wig, sleep eyes, inset lashes, 30", $650-$750.

PEGGY LOU
Composition, closed mouth, painted eyes, 20", $950-
$1,150.

ROSEMARY—1925
Cloth body, composition head, arms, legs, shoulders; hair
or mohair wig, tin sleep eyes, opened mouth (see Chapter
4, "Black Composition Dolls")—14", $200-$250; 17",
$300-$350; 25", $400-$450; 30", $500 and up.

SUZETTE—1939
Composition, painted eyes, 11 1/2", $200.

SWEETIE PIE
Composition, sleep eyes, lashes, wig, 18", $150.

TOMMY TUCKER
Composition, flirty eyes, painted hair or mohair wig, cloth
body, 16"-18", $225; 22"-24", $325.

PATSY RUTH
Composition, wig, sleep eyes, inset lashes, 26", $600-$700. Courtesy of Lynnae
Ramsey.

WEE PATSY
Composition, molded and painted hair,
painted eyes, painted shoes and socks,
6", $250-$275.

SUZANNE—1940
Composition, 14", $275.
Courtesy of Sunnie Newell.

SKIPPY—1928

All composition, some were made with cloth body and composition arms, legs, and head; molded and painted hair; chubby toddler-type cheeks; small, closed mouth; painted eyes with side glancing look; Patsy body, 14", $400-$550.

Far Right: Skippy with book, composition with painted features, 14", $450-$500. Courtesy of Sunnie Newell.

Right: Army Skippy with cloth body and painted boots. The brown paint on boots goes up leg. $450 and up. Courtesy of Pat Wood.

11" Effanbee Patricia Kin shown with an excellent example of the 14" Skippy Aviator. Patricia Kin sold at McMaster's 1998 Doll Auction for $1,100. The old story about supply and demand came true in this case. The Skippy Aviator is a sought-after doll, and it's difficult to find him in such great condition. This piece sold at McMaster's 1998 Doll Auction for $3,200 (usual price, $750-$1,000).

Right: 14" Effanbee Black Skippy, a rare find and all original. Sold at McMaster's 1998 Doll Auction for $1,350.

CHAPTER SIX
HUSTLER TOY COMPANY

According to collectors James and Judy Sneed, noted collectors of a great variety of wood pull toys, the Hustler Toy Co. was a subsidiary of Frantz Manufacturing Co., of Sterling Illinois. Frantz started the business in 1909, and is continuing to this day making garage door parts. Frantz started making toys in the early 1920s, and stopped by 1936. Several of their early toys can be found marked "Frantz"—and later, "Hustler." They manufactured about 100 different toy models, including pull toys, baseball and football games, roller skates, and construction sets. Clarence A. Wetzell was the inventor of most of the toy designs. Pricing these toys in today's market is very difficult since there are few examples of prices realized. (The majority of these toys can be picked up from the $50 to $100 range, though I see potential for increases as more collectors become familiar with these wonderfully made toys. I would price black character pieces in the $100-$200 range.)

Hustler Bellhop. This hard-to-find piece shows a black bellhop with black bags in hand upon a yellow base with blue wheels. He is wearing a red uniform with red hat, all wood with painted features; metal piece holds body to base and bags in hand; $200-$275. Courtesy of James & Judy Sneed.

The Hustler Toy Company's Hustler Twins, all wood with painted features, hands connected to move when string is pulled, with original box. Without box, $100-$150; with box, add $75. Courtesy of James & Judy Sneed.

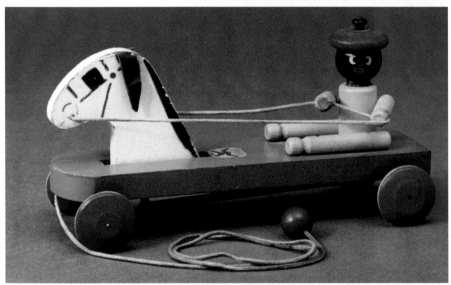

Above: Hustler Toy Company's Hiram, also known as Hiram Hustler, red base with yellow wheels, painted features, all wood, white horse with black ears screwed into sides of head; arms go up and down as string is pulled; $100-$150. Courtesy of James & Judy Sneed.

Left: Hustler Toy Company's Sambo and his Mule. Horse is identical to Hiram Hustler; this piece has green base with red wheels, Sambo has yellow body with black head and painted features; atop his head sits a red hat with black top piece; original label on base, $200-$250. Courtesy of James & Judy Sneed.

Betty Roll Duck in various colors. Made by Hustler Toy Company, these cute little ducks came in an array of colors including different colors on base, painted eyes and feathers, wheels attached to body with metal, $75 each. Courtesy of James & Judy Sneed.

Close-up of Sambo, string goes through the hand pieces to make arms move when string is pulled. Courtesy of James & Judy Sneed.

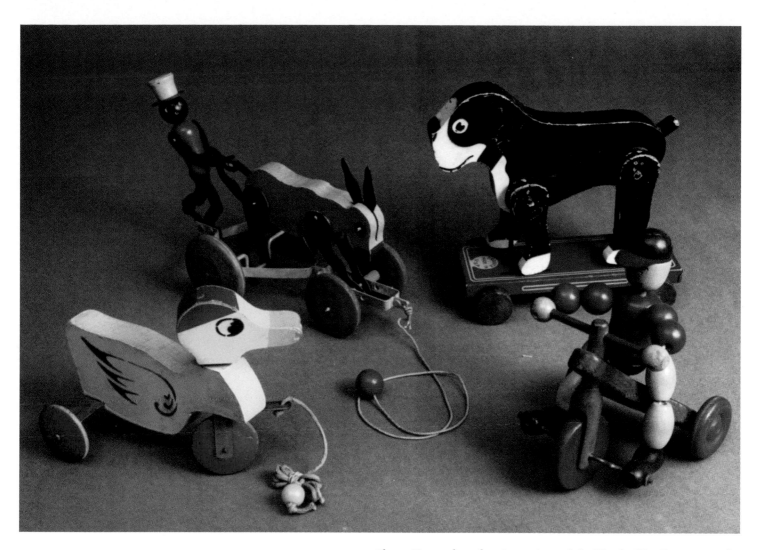

Above: Group shot of various toys made by Hustler Toy Company and Frantz Manufacturing. The Boy Doll on the bicycle is unmarked and his origin unknown. Courtesy of James & Judy Sneed.

Left: Close-up of Betty Roll Duck. Hustler Toy Company, which manufactured the ducks, was a division of Frantz manufacturing; $75. Courtesy of James & Judy Sneed.

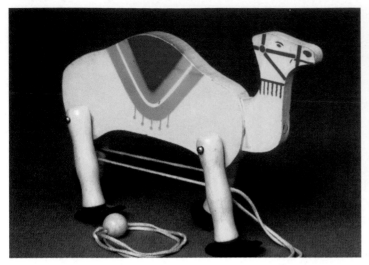

Hustler Toy Company's Walking Camel. Yellow with red painted features and black feet, this pull toy walks when pulled by string; $75-$100. Courtesy of James & Judy Sneed.

Hustler Toy Company's Billy is directing his dog where to take him. Dog is white with black painted features, and red wheels; Billy is sitting on a green base with pink wheels—his arms are jointed to move up and down as the string is pulled (string is connected through dog's mouth), $150. Courtesy of James & Judy Sneed.

Frantz Toys created this great piece called "Fran-zell the Dog." Used as an Atlantic City advertising piece, Fran-zell was the walking, barking dog. All wood with black and white body on red base with yellow striping, red wheels; shown here with original box, $150-$175 (if not marked "Atlantic City," $75-$100). Courtesy of James & Judy Sneed.

This Duck by Toylander of Sterling, Illinois, drinks as he is pulled along. It is believed that Hustler Toy Company bought Toylander, a company with similar production capabilities. This duck is yellow with an orange bill and feet; he has painted eyes and feathers—and sits upon a green base with yellow wheels; the bowl is metal, $75. Courtesy of James & Judy Sneed.

Hustler Toy Company's Hustler Watch Dog. Using a base that was used for other toys, this dog has his very own dog house in green and white. Original label on base of toy, red base with yellow wheels, the black features are painted on this little doggy; $125-$150. Courtesy of James & Judy Sneed.

Hustler Toy Company's Poncho Hustler, sits upon a black base with oversized horse head in front, large green wheels, with dog in rear, $150-$200. Courtesy of James & Judy Sneed.

Right: Close-up of Poncho Hustler with yellow body and red circles; string is run through red balls that act as hands for this pull toy. Jointed at legs. Courtesy of James & Judy Sneed.

Wonderfully rare Deanna Durbin, 25", exquisite and all original, $1,500 and up. Courtesy of Pat Wood.

CHAPTER SEVEN
THE IDEAL TOY CORPORATION AND THE SHIRLEY TEMPLE DOLLS

In 1903, Morris Mitchtom and his wife began their tiny business by producing a pair of teddy bears. They sold the bears out of their stationery store in Brooklyn, New York. The teddy bears were an instant success, and the Mitchtoms began producing more and more bears. From this, the Ideal Novelty and Toy Company was born. The Ideal Novelty and Toy Company began producing dolls, and over the years produced some of the country's most popular ones. In the 1930s, the company secured rights to produce a doll after one of the most popular little stars of the time: Shirley Temple. The 1930s and 1940s were times of great growth for the company—producing such winners, along with Shirley Temple, as the Deanna Durbin Doll and the Judy Garland Doll, to name a few. The baby-boomer dolls were produced in the 1950s with such hits as the Toni® Doll with the Toni home permanents. This doll was one of the most popular dolls of the 1950s.

Toni is a registered trademark of the Gillette Co.

Deanna Durbin, all original, 21", $500-$600. Courtesy of Lynnae Ramsey.

FERDINAND THE BULL
Composition Ferdinand the Bull with a flower coming out of his mouth, butterfly marking on back by tail, Disney character, $175-$250. Author's Collection.

HOWDY DOODY—1940S
(© Bob Smith)
Howdy Doody, manufactured by Ideal Toy and Novelty Company, but designed by Joseph Kallus. Composition and wood-jointed with painted features, chest decal, leather belt, bandanna around neck, $550-$750. Author's Collection.

GABBY FROM GULLIVER'S TRAVELS
Gabby, 11", composition and wood-jointed, $450-$600. Courtesy of Carl Kludt.

FLEXIES—1938-1942
Composition with wire limbs, Baby Snooks (Fanny Brice), Mortimer Snerd both made in 1938, Soldier (1938), Clown (1938), Sam or Sunny Sue, all 12"-13", $195-$295.

Below: Flexy Soldier, $200-$225. Courtesy of Carl Kludt.

Above Left & Right: Mortimer Snerd, part of the Flexy series. His legs and arms are made out of a thick, flexible wire; composition head, hands, and feet; torso is made of a metal mesh; $200-$275. Author's Collection.

Right: Fanny Brice, also known as Baby Snooks, composition hands and feet, molded head with a wire body, $200-$275. Author's Collection.

Jiminy Cricket—1939-1940
Top Left & Above: Composition and wood-segmented body; a Walt Disney Design. Jiminy Cricket, 10", all original, including hat, excellent condition, $750 and up. Author's Collection.

Smaller version of Jiminy Cricket, 7", composition and wood-jointed, painted features, $275-$375. Author's Collection.

Humphrey Mobile
This group shot shows an Ideal composition and cloth-stuffed doll of "Humphrey Mobile" from the "Joe Palooka" comic strip. Humphrey with painted, smiling face; black, vinyl hands; wearing large, felt clothes; cap atop his red hair, 14 1/2", $450-$600. Included in this photo is a boxed set of Little Orphan Annie with Sandy (Annie, 12"; Sandy, 7"; $500-$750; not Ideal Toys). Courtesy of Christie's Images.

JUDY GARLAND—1939
Dorothy of the Wizard of Oz, *all composition, all original, 14", $500-$800; 16", $900-$1,100; 18", $750-$1,200. Dolls made from 1941 on, 14", $175-$295; 21", $375-$500.*

Above: Rare Judy Garland Doll, 21". Marked "21," this doll was also used as "Miss Liberty" and was made with the lighter hair for only one year. All original, $800 and up. Courtesy of Pat Wood.

Judy Garland Doll, Marked "15, Ideal Doll, made in USA" on back of head, "USA, 16" on back. Composition character head, large brown sleep eyes, real lashes, eye shadow, opened mouth with four upper teeth, original human hair wig, five-piece composition child body. Dressed in original dress with white organdy top, blue-and-white check dress with white buttons, blue hair ribbons, 15", $1,000-$2,000, shown here with Cowardly Lion. Courtesy of McMaster's Doll Auctions (sold at McMaster's Auction in 1996 for $2,800).

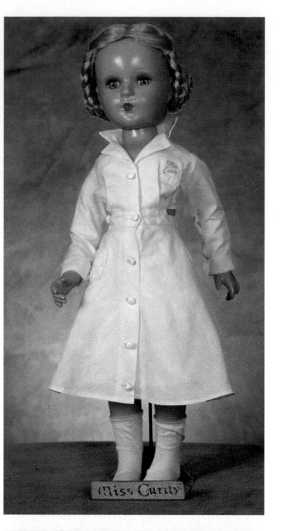

MISS CURITY
Above: Miss Curity, with original stand and uniform, all composition with blue sleep eyes, jointed legs and arms, blonde mohair wig, with original stand and uniform, 19", $575 and up; 14", $400. Author's Collection.

Bottom Right: Miss Curity with ads advertising the Curity Band-Aids. In one ad it advertises the fact that your daughter can enter to be the model for the new "Miss Curity" and she could win $5,000. Every little girl that entered received a Miss Curity nurse's cap. Author's Collection.

LIBERTY BOY—1918
Composition, 12", $150-$225. Courtesy of Carl Kludt.

Far Left: UNEEDA BISCUIT BOY Advertising doll for National Biscuit Company. Unmarked, yellow slicker has tag on right sleeve. Composition head, painted blue eyes, closed mouth, molded and painted shoes and stockings; 15", $250-$400. Courtesy of Annette's Antique Dolls.

SNOW WHITE—1937
Snow White and Seven Dwarfs. Each stuffed doll is cloth-dressed, named, and has a painted composition face. Values include original boxes for Dwarfs. Snow White, 15 1/2" with Dwarfs, 7" $2,000-$3,000. Other all-composition, jointed, opened mouth Snow White dolls include 11"-13" model, $350-$450; 18" model, $500-$600; and a model with molded black hair and painted blue bow, 13"-14", $175-$225. Courtesy of Christie's Images.

PINOCCHIO—1938-1941
(For other photos, see Chapter 3, "Disney Dolls & Toys")
Composition and wood-jointed, front and back view of Pinocchio, 12", $275-$325. Courtesy of Sunnie Newell.

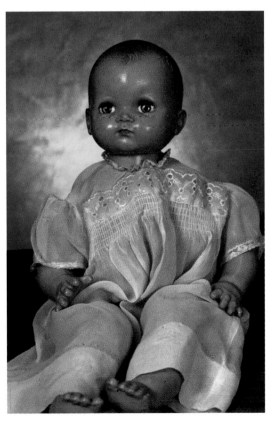

UNEEDA KID—1914-1919
Composition head, molded hair, painted blue eyes, molded black boots on composition legs, cloth body, 16", $375-$450; 24", $575-$650.

Baby with composition arms and legs with hard plastic head and cloth body, sleep eyes, closed mouth, 21", $150-$175. Author's Collection.

SUPERMAN
A Joseph Kallus creation, this Superman was made by the Ideal Toy & Novelty Company. Wood-jointed with cape, body is jointed in center. Molded and painted head, painted features, 13", $1,000 and up (can go as high as $2,000 with box). Courtesy of Robert Greene.

OTHER IDEAL DOLLS NOT PICTURED

BETSY WETSY—1937-1940
Composition head, rubber body, 13", $65-$110; 16", $75-$125.

BETTY JANE—1930-1943
All composition, sleep eyes, opened mouth, Shirley Temple look-alike, 14", $150-$250; 16", $175-275; 24", $200-$300.

BROTHER-BABY COOS—1951
Cloth and composition with hard plastic head, 25", $75-$120; composition head with latex body, 24", $65-$100.

FLOSSIE FLIRT—1938-1945
Composition and cloth, flirty eyes, 16", $150-$200; 20", $175-$250; 24", $250-$350; Black version, $250-$375; Boy, 17", $150-$250.

KING LITTLE—1939
Composition and wood combination, 14", $450-$600. (See Chapter 1, "The Cameo Doll Company & Joseph Kallus")

MAGIC SKIN BABY—1940s
Came with composition or hard plastic head with cloth body, latex rubber body and limbs, 14", $75-$100; 17", $150-$175.

MAMA DOLLS—1920-1930s
Composition head with cloth body; 14", $150-$200; 16", $150-$225; 18", $175-$275; 24", $200-$300.

MARY JANE
All composition, sleep eyes, opened mouth, marked "Ideal," 18", $250-$275; 21", $200-$300.

MISS USO—1940s, ALSO USED AS MISS LIBERTY
Used the Judy Garland/Deanna Durbin Doll, all Caucasian blonde wig, sleep eyes. During World War II this doll was used as Miss America and as a Red Cross Nurse, 12", $300-$375; 14", $425-$575; 18", $650-$800; 21", $950 and up.

PLASSIE—1942
Cloth body, composition head, 14", $125-$150; 22", $225-$275.

SALLY-SALLYKINS—1934
Composition and cloth combination, two upper and lower teeth, flirty eyes, 14", $75-$125; 19", $125-$200; 25", $125-$250.

SHIRLEY TEMPLE—1930s AND ON
11", $750-$850; 13", $750-$900; 15"-16", $750-$900; 18", $900-1,000; 20"-22", $1,000-$1,200; 25", $1,100-$1,300. (See pp. 91-99 for more information.)

SNOOZIE—1933
Composition head; sleep eyes; molded hair; cloth body; arms and legs could be composition or rubber; 13", $165-$195; 16", $175-$250; 20", $250-$300.

TICKLETOES—1930s
Composition and cloth; 15", $95-$125; 21", $125-$220.

Flirty-eyed Shirley, composition, 25", $1,000 and up. Susan Killoran Collection.

Shirley Temple with doll in carriage. Author's Collection.

Shirley Temple ad with composition doll. Author's Collection.

Cereal premiums offered by General Mills' Wheaties in 1938. Shirley Temple cobalt-blue cereal bowl, pitcher, and mug; $75-$125. Susan Killoran Collection.

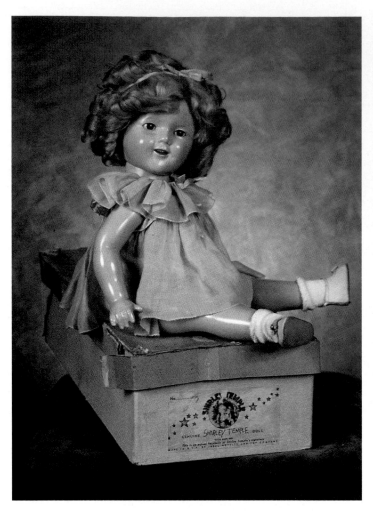

Shirley Temple, 18", in original outfit with her original box, $1,000 and up. Susan Killoran Collection.

Shirley Temple, 18", in her original outfit, $800-$1,000. Susan Killoran Collection.

Left: Shirley Temple, 18". Look at those pink knees! Susan Killoran Collection.

Shirley Temple, 18", Susan Killoran Collection.

Shirley Temple, 18", with pin, $800-$1,000. Susan Killoran Collection.

Left: Shirley Temple, 18", from Wee Willie Winkie, $850-$1,000. Courtesy of Susan Killoran Collection.

Shirley Temple, 18", in skating outfit. Susan Killoran Collection.

Shirley Temple, 13". Susan Killoran Collection.

Shirley Temple, 20", $900-$1,000 with original clothes. Susan Killoran Collection.

Shirley Temple, 18", in her original outfit, $800-$1,000. Susan Killoran Collection.

Group shot of Shirleys. Susan Killoran Collection.

Shirley Temple, 22", $1,000 and up. Susan Killoran Collection.

Shirley Temple, 20", $900-$1,000. Susan Killoran Collection.

Shirley, 25", in original red dress, $1,200. Courtesy of Lynnae Ramsey.

Beautiful Shirley Temple, 11", $600-$700. Courtesy of Lynnae Ramsey.

Left: All original, 22" Shirley Temple, $1,000 and up. Courtesy of Lynnae Ramsey.

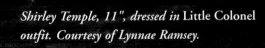

Shirley Temple, 11", dressed in Little Colonel *outfit. Courtesy of Lynnae Ramsey.*

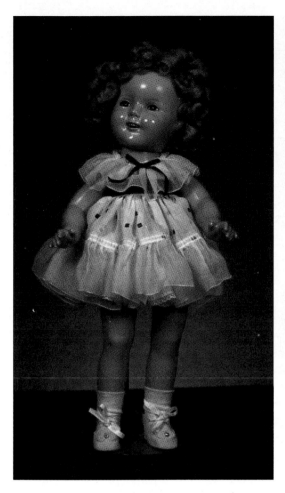

Shirley Temple with blue and white dress, all original, 20", $900-$1,000. Courtesy of Lynnae Ramsey.

Shirley Temple in blue dress, 16", $650-$750. Courtesy of Lynnae Ramsey.

Shirley Temple in red and white dress, 16", $650-$750. Courtesy of Lynnae Ramsey.

Left: Shirley Temple Baby, 18", all original with flirty eyes, $1,000 and up. Courtesy of Pat Wood.

Right: Hawaiian Shirley, excellent example, all original, $800-$900.

Canada's version of the Shirley Temple Doll, 29", original dress which came with a hat, $600-$750. Courtesy of Pat Wood.

BRIGHT EYES—*1934*
22", with aviator jacket and helmet; rare, $1,500 and up.

CAPTAIN JANUARY—*1936*
16", $850; 18", $950; 20", $1,000 and up; flirty eyes; organdy dress with blue and white flowers.

CURLY TOP—*1935*
22", dressed in velveteen coat and hat, white organdy pleated dress; from $1,000 and up; with trunk and outfits, including roller and ice skates, $1,500.

NOW & FOREVER—*1934*
18"; dress is green, lavender, orange and red; $950-$1,000.

OUR LITTLE GIRL—*1935*
13", Scotty dogs on dress, $850-$900, 18"; $1,000 and up.

POOR LITTLE RICH GIRL—*1936*
20", dressed in sailor dress; $1,000 and up.

Shirley Temple, 27", from **Bright Eyes,** *all original, $1,500. Courtesy of Lynnae Ramsey.*

Shirley Temple, 13", with many outfits, all original, $1,000 and up. Courtesy of Pat Wood.

Shirley Temple in aviator's outfit. Courtesy of Pat Wood.

Two of the many Shirley Temple books produced.

LITTLE COLONEL
Here we have a 13" ($900-$1,000) and a 22" ($1,100-$1,300)
Shirley Temple Doll in the Little Colonial outfit, all original.

Ranger Shirley, 18", all original, $1,500 and up. Courtesy
of Lynnae Ramsey.

MARILYN KNOWLDEN
This Shirley was a meant-to-be
Shirley; however, Shirley Temple
did not authorize the release of
this doll. It was produced as
Marilyn Knowlden from the movie
Imitation of Life, 1935. Marked
"USA" on back, "Ideal Doll USA"
on head, all original (not enough
examples to price), 13", $400-
$500. Courtesy of Pat Wood.

Shirley Temple Ranger, with box, marked "Shirley
Temple, Cop Ideal N & T Co." on head, Shirley
Temple tag on red bandanna, original Shirley
Temple button, Shirley Temple label on end of box
lid; composition head, hazel sleep eyes with real
lashes, opened mouth with six upper teeth, original
mohair wig, five-piece composition body. Dressed in
original tagged Ranger outfit, red plaid shirt, red
bandanna, khaki shorts, brown leather chaps, vest
with red decorations, red/blue imitation leather hol-
ster and belt, silver gun marked "G Man," socks and
brown imitation leather boots; 17", $2,000-$3,000.
Courtesy of McMaster's Doll Auction (Sold for
$5,000 at 1996 McMaster's Auction).

*This Jaymar Occident Flour Man is a rare advertising piece. Red and white with baker's hat, 6", with "Occident" across chest; also has the Occident logo on body with "Costs More * Worth It," $150-$250. Courtesy of Dan Sumpter.*

CHAPTER EIGHT
JAYMAR SPECIALTY COMPANY

The Jaymar Specialty Company was based at 200 5th Ave., New York City, and produced a variety of wood-jointed figures, including many character pieces. The prices range from $50-$100 for the smaller non-character pieces, and $75-$150 for most of the smaller character toys. Some of the more sought-after pieces can go as high as $225. Sears was a major distributor for the Jaymar Company, and the majority of their pieces were produced in the 1920s and 1930s.

Two sizes of the Jaymar Little Orphan Annie, 5" and 5 3/4", marked "Little Orphan Annie, Harold Gray," red and white with red and white cap, painted features, $100-$150. Courtesy of Dan Sumpter.

Little Orphan Annie, $100-$125. Courtesy of Gasoline Alley.

Close-up of Popeye family including Popeye, Olive Oyl, Jeep, and Wimpy, $75-$125 each. Courtesy of Gasoline Alley.

A truly rare find in the original box, this set came complete with all the pieces to make the whole Popeye Family, with box, $750-$1,000 plus. Courtesy of Gasoline Alley.

Olive Oyl at 4 3/4", Wimpy at 4 1/2", she is wearing a red blouse with black skirt, yellow legs and orange feet, features are hand-painted, and she is marked "Olive Oyl c. K.F.S." which stands for King Features Syndicate. He is wearing a black jacket with white shirt, orange legs with black shoes, and with his signature orange cap. Courtesy of Dan Sumpter.

Wimpy by Jaymar in another color combination of orange and black, $75-$100. Courtesy of Gasoline Alley.

Two sizes of the Jaymar Popeye, 4 3/4" and 5 3/4". They are different both in coloring and in shape. The smaller Popeye has yellow shoes; the larger Popeye has black shoes. $125-$175. Courtesy of Dan Sumpter.

Rare Jaymar oversized Popeye, at 8 1/2", possibly used as a salesman's sample. Blue shirt, green pants, black shoes, with red collar; pipe hangs out of his mouth, $350 and up. Courtesy of Dan Sumpter.

Jaymar Andy and Amos; Andy is 6 1/4"; same description as on page 105, but notice difference in color of hat. Many times pieces were interchanged for different characters, so you can find the same character with different colors of feet, hats, etc. Amos is 6 1/2", wearing his red hat marked "Taxi," black and white top with green pants, $150-$225 each. Courtesy of Dan Sumpter.

Two sizes of the Jaymar Joe Palooka dolls, 4" and 5 3/4". Both are identical with red boxer shorts, gloves on hands, and the words "Joe Palooka" across chest, $125-$175. Courtesy of Dan Sumpter.

Puss'n'Boots, wood-jointed with black boots with red trim, white collar, orange body, all wood-jointed, 3 1/2", $100-$150; 8", $250-$300. Courtesy of Dan Sumpter.

Unmarked Dog, similar to the Jaymar styling, 5 1/4" long, all wood with red body, white tail and paws, with blue legs and yellow head, painted features, $25-$40. Courtesy of Ronnie Kauk.

Jaymar Andy marked "Andy Correll & Gosden," all wood-jointed with green body, yellow pants and hat, black shoes, cigar hangs out of his mouth, painted features, $150-$225. Courtesy of Ronnie Kauk.

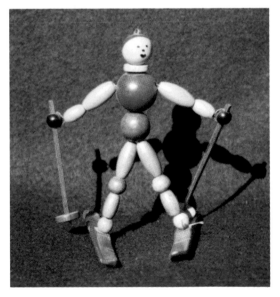

All wood Charlie McCarthy, unmarked but similar to the Jaymar pieces, 5 1/2", all black with white shirt and black top hat, Fun-E-Flex type arms, $100-$150. Nice character piece. Courtesy of Ronnie Kauk.

The Little Pig, all wood, 3", red body with green feet; tan arms, legs and head; red hat; $50-$75. Courtesy of Ronnie Kauk.

Skier, all wood, 3", made in Czechoslovakia, labeled on ski. This is not a Jaymar piece, but very similar, $25-$50. Courtesy of Ronnie Kauk.

Ignatz from "Krazy Kat," 5 1/2", unmarked but believed to be made by Jaymar. Black and white with large ears and long nose. Felt, wire-type tail, $150-$225. Courtesy of Dan Sumpter.

Jaymar Jiggs, from "Bringing Up Father," great character piece, marked "Jiggs" on stomach, wearing a black suit with white dickie, nice painted features on face, cane in left hand, black top hat, $125-$150. Courtesy of Dan Sumpter.

Jaymar Daffy Duck, a Warner Brothers piece. Marked "Daffy Duck-Warner Brothers" on foot; 6", black body with yellow legs and beak; large, painted, white eyes. A nice character piece; $150-$225. Courtesy of Dan Sumpter.

Two sizes of the Jaymar Moon Mullins, 4 3/4" and 5 3/4"; wearing his signature cap in orange; black suit with orange tie; one has green arms, while the smaller version has black arms; green pants; cigar hanging from mouth; large smile with painted features; $100-$150. Courtesy of Dan Sumpter.

Jaymar Kayo, Moon Mullins's side kick, 4", black top hat, red body and arms with green pants and black shoes. Hand-painted features show his mad expression, $100-$150. Courtesy of Dan Sumpter.

Jaymar Moon Mullins, 5 1/2", all wood-jointed with orange top hat; large, painted smile; cigar, blue jacket, and green pants; $100-$150. Courtesy of Ronnie Kauk.

Jaymar Ed Wynn in two sizes: 4 1/2" and 5 3/4". Ed Wynn had an early television show; marked "USA," he is wearing his red fireman's suit, with red hat marked "Fire Chief;" his body is marked "Ed Wynn;" the larger version has a felt bow tie while the smaller version has a painted bow tie; he is holding a shovel in his right hand, $125-$150. Courtesy of Dan Sumpter.

Jaymar Jester, large red hat with yellow ball on top, green felt trim around waist and neck, $25-$50.

Jaymar China Man, 6", yellow face, hands and feet; black pants, red and white top with red and white cap; oriental painted features, $50-$75. Courtesy of Dan Sumpter.

Jaymar Soldier from "Parade of the Wooden Soldier," 6 1/2", red hat with red jacket, blue pants with black shoes, carrying his necessities on his back, $50-$75. Courtesy of Dan Sumpter.

Jaymar Policeman, 5 3/4", wearing blue uniform with blue hat, painted features with large smile; he has baton in his right hand. Many times the rubber bands that hold these pieces together become brittle and crack and need to be replaced. When this piece was restrung, his legs were put on upside down, $50-$75. Courtesy of Dan Sumpter.

Hard-to-find Jaymar Indian, 6 1/2", a colorful piece with his green top, blue pants, and his headpiece in multi-colors, $100-$125. Courtesy of Dan Sumpter.

Jaymar Rooster, 6 1/2", very colorful with blue body, green tail; yellow legs, neck, and beak; orange head with painted features and red feathers on top, $50-$75. Courtesy of Dan Sumpter.

Another version of the Jaymar Indian at 6 3/4", marked "made in USA" (notice extra piece in leg.) Holding tomahawk in right hand, $100-$125. Courtesy of Ronnie Kauk.

Jaymar Bear and Elephant; bear is 4", blue body with orange legs and brown head; he has a molded nose with two round ears and painted features; the elephant is 3 1/2", all red except for yellow on back; long, jointed trunk with tusks and black wood ears, $25-$50 each. Courtesy of Dan Sumpter.

Jaymar Sandy, Little Orphan Annie's dog, 3 3/4", orange with painted features and large smile, $50-$75. Courtesy of Dan Sumpter.

Jaymar Gator, 5 3/4", long stout, green body, orange limbs and head; green hat; has a very unhappy look painted on his face, $50-$75. Courtesy of Dan Sumpter.

Jaymar Giraffe, 6 1/2", long neck all in orange except for feet and ears, felt tail. All wood-jointed, $50-$75. Courtesy of Dan Sumpter.

Jaymar Ostrich, 5 3/4", all wood with red body, orange neck, yellow head and legs with black feet and tail, $50-$75. Courtesy of Dan Sumpter.

German-style "Pinocchio" unmarked but Jaymar type. Wood-jointed features with pointed nose and tall, white hat; green body with red and yellow legs, large brown feet, $50-$75. Courtesy of Dan Sumpter.

Humpty Dumpty by Jaymar, 5", a happy, colorful fellow with red body; tan and red, jointed limbs; orange legs and black shoes; green hat, green felt trim around neck. He was used as part of a Christmas ornament package, $50-$75. Courtesy of Dan Sumpter.

Red Goose, wood jointed, marked "Made in USA" on foot, yellow beak and feet, red body and neck, $50-$75. Courtesy of Ronnie Kauk.

A boxed Jaymar set of Make Your Own Funnies, containing wood-jointed figures of Popeye, Chinaman, Komical Kop, Orphan Annie, Sandy, Kayo, Indian, Funny Frog, Comical Mouse, and Moon Mullins. Figures are 5" tall, $800-$1,200. Courtesy of Christie's Images.

Jaymar Ring-A-Ling set (Circus); 5 3/4" multicolored Clown, 4 1/2" brown Donkey, 2 1/2" yellow Pig; a great set with many of the circus pieces, $350. Courtesy of Dan Sumpter.

Jaymar-type Minnie Mouse, original clothes, all wood, painted features, missing ears, stick legs, ball arms, $50-$75. Courtesy of Ronnie Kauk.

Snowman, marked "USA" on foot, all white with black hat and red nose, $25-$50. Unusual piece. Courtesy of Ronnie Kauk.

Sailor at 4 1/2", dark blue uniform with blue cap, painted face with mustache. The hook on the top of his head was used to make the piece a Christmas ornament which several of the Jaymar toys were used for; $50-$75. Courtesy of Dan Sumpter.

Jaymar-style Man. Another unusual piece because of his size—10" tall. Green body and arms with black lower section and large orange feet, small brown hat on head. Painted features are different from the other Jaymar characters, $100-$125. Courtesy of Dan Sumpter.

Jaymar Little King with original box, 3 3/4" tall, box reads "Pull string out of Little King's hat, place Little King on a smooth surface, release string and watch him travel." Box marked "Jaymar Made in USA 200 Fifth Ave. NY," $150-$225. Courtesy of Davis Ingraham.

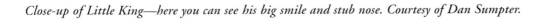

Close-up of Little King—here you can see his big smile and stub nose. Courtesy of Dan Sumpter.

A different look from Kohner, this pull toy is made of larger wood pieces. Jointed at arms and legs, the balls hit the bell when the toy is pulled along. Great piece. Courtesy of James & Judy Sneed.

CHAPTER NINE
KOHNER BROTHERS

The Kohner Brothers manufactured a large variety of plastic and wood-jointed toys, as well as all wood toys. Most of the pop-up pieces run in the $25 to $50 range, with a few of the harder-to-find pieces and Disney pieces going for up to $150. Still relatively inexpensive collectibles, the pushups are marked with the name of the piece, a patent number, and the words "A KOHNER PRODUCT." They range in size from 5" to 6 1/2". The pushup toys were called "Push-Button PUPPETS, Funny-Lovable-Animated Characters." The boxes read, "Just press button at bottom of base—watch puppets spring to life . . . to delight the young and old." The Kohner push-ups were a common childhood toy. The Disney pieces were introduced in the 1950s; however, they were still being produced up until 1977. The majority of the toys were produced from Cartoon Characters or Character Personalities. A large variety of animals were also popular. In 1970, Kohner Brothers was acquired by Kraft General Foods Inc., of Glenview, Illinois, in their attempt to diversify. Five years later, they were sold to Gabriel Industries. Early information on the company has been hard to obtain—contact with anyone who has such information would be greatly appreciated.

Kohner pushup #180, Howdy Doody© Bob Smith, wood-jointed with plastic base, painted features, felt piece around neck, "NBC" marked on microphone, $75-$100. Courtesy of Dan Sumpter.

Kohner pushup #125 Bronco Bill, wood-jointed with brown, jointed horse; yellow saddle and cowboy in red outfit with blue cowboy hat; painted features on horse and cowboy; he is carrying a stick in right hand; $25-$50. Courtesy of Ronnie Kauk.

Kohner pushup #182, wood-jointed horse with Lone Ranger atop; he wears a black outfit with white hat; horse is all white; they sit on plastic base, $50-$75. Courtesy of Ronnie Kauk.

Kohner pushup #140, 5" Donkey, wood-jointed with plastic base; donkey has red body with yellow tail and head; yellow and black, jointed legs; painted features; felt ears; $25-$50. Courtesy of Ronnie Kauk.

Kohner pushup #141, Peter Pan with original box, Peter is made of green, beaded wood, with white arms; he holds a large white sword in right hand; great features; green hat with feather, $75; without box, $50. Courtesy of Ronnie Kauk.

Kohner pushup #131, 5 1/2" Pluto, another WDP piece; Pluto is yellow with black feet and tail; black, painted features with black nose; sitting on red, plastic base, $50-$75. Courtesy of Ronnie Kauk.

Kohner pushup #176, Indian Chief, wood-jointed brown horse with yellow Indian on top, sitting on yellow saddle and carrying hacket in left hand, painted features on horse and Indian, $50. Courtesy of Ronnie Kauk.

Left: Kohner pushup of Walt Disney's Davy Crockett (Fess Parker), 6", wood-jointed with plastic base. Davy is wearing a brown suit with buckskin hat and carrying his gun. Painted features; painted details on shirt; paper label that reads, "Walt Disney is OFFICIAL DAVY CROCKETT" (FESS PARKER) c. Walt Disney Productions, a Kohner Product with patent number, $50-$75. Courtesy of Ronnie Kauk.

Right: Kohner pushup #121, Hit & Miss, wood-jointed Boxers; one with yellow trunks, one with green trunks; on plastic base; $25-$50. Courtesy of Ronnie Kauk.

Kohner #132, 5 3/4" Tipsy Tom. Wearing a black tuxedo, black top hat, and holding on to lamppost; bottle in opposite hand, $25-$50. Courtesy of Ronnie Kauk.

Unmarked Santa Claus, wood-jointed with green wood base, bell and sack in right hand, felt type hat and beard, painted features, 7", shows U.S. patent number, probably made by Kohner, $25-$50. Courtesy of Ronnie Kauk.

Kohner pushup #126, Mac the Sailor, all wood with plastic base, yellow wheel with hands connected, smiling face, painted features, blue sailor uniform with white sailor's cap, $25-$50. Courtesy of Ronnie Kauk.

Kohner pushup #139, Elephant, all wood, including base; leather ears, braided tail, $25-$50. Courtesy of Ronnie Kauk.

Kohner pushup #139; this Elephant is the same as the previous elephant, except it's on a plastic base; also, the trunk has two extra beads on the end making it longer, $25-$50. Courtesy of Dan Sumpter.

Left: Kohner pushup #128, c.W.D.P., a Walt Disney piece, Donald Duck. Donald is at the wheel of his ship; he is wearing a blue suit and hat and holding a white wheel with the words "Donald Duck" in red, $75-$125. Courtesy of Ronnie Kauk.

Right: Kohner pushup #136, Princess Summerfall Winterspring, Robert E. Smith, 6", very cute Princess with black hair, mouth that opens and closes, multicolored beaded arms attached to drum, wearing a felt skirt with felt collar, painted features with eyes to side, $50-$75. Courtesy of Dan Sumpter.

LOONEY LINKS

These photos show the container for Loony Links. Enclosed are various wood pieces that can be pushed together to create different animals and people, $75-$100. Author's Collection.

The Drunk, another Kohner pushup, 6 1/2", painted features, red wood base; body is solid piece of wood, while legs are made up of black beads. He holds bottle in one hand with second bottle at base; $50-$75. Courtesy of Dan Sumpter.

Kohner pushup #153, Lucky the Cat, 6", wood-jointed, plastic base; all black with yellow paws; white painted features; round, wooden body; $25-$50. Courtesy of Dan Sumpter.

Kohner pushup #177,
similar FLUB-A-DUB
as on page 125, except
the features and neck
are different. This one
sports a yellow felt bow
tie; $50-$75. Courtesy
of Dan Sumpter.

*Kohner pushup of Rudolph the Reindeer, 5 1/2";
plastic base with light-brown, golden body and legs;
hoofs are black; felt ears with red, wooden nose;
$25-$50. Courtesy of Dan Sumpter.*

*Kohner pushup #185, Mickey Mouse, ©Walt Disney Productions, wood-joint-
ed with plastic base, large ears, painted features. Mickey's body is red and
black with orange feet; his yellow and red drum is held up with wire; $75-
$100.*

*Kohner pushup #177, FLUB-A-DUB, Howdy
Doody's Pal, © Bob Smith, 5", wood-jointed
with mouth that opens and closes, blue spots
on neck, light blue hat, felt ears; $50-$75.
Courtesy of Ronnie Kauk.*

Sonja Henie in black outfit, all original, 21". Courtesy of Pat Wood.

CHAPTER TEN
MADAME ALEXANDER DOLL COMPANY
& THE DIONNE QUINTUPLETS

The Madame Alexander Doll Company—whose dolls have been made out of composition, cloth, wood, vinyl, and hard plastic—was started in 1912 by Beatrice and Rose Alexander. Their expertise was in designing doll costumes. And, in 1928, the trademark "Madame Alexander" was launched. It was the marketing genius of Madame Alexander that helped the company's success by retaining marketing rights to many successful personality dolls—such as the Dionne Quintuplets. Here is a brief history of the Dionne children and the dolls they inspired.

On May 28, 1934, in Callender, Ontario, Canada, the quintuplet babies were born. The mother, Elzire Dionne, was just 25 years old. Her family went from 7 to 12 in one day.

The weight of all the babies combined totaled 10 pounds, 1 1/4 ounces, and not one of the little angels was longer than 9". The infants were placed in a basket to keep them warm, but no one expected the babies to live. Up to that date, no quintuplets had ever survived—and, there weren't many things going in the Dionne's favor: Their home, where they were born, was old and broken down. There were no screens on the windows, no running water, not even any electricity. How was a young mother to care for these infants?

The Chicago World's Fair was just around the corner, and the father of these babies was looking for ways to support his newly enlarged family. He was offered a large sum of money to put the babies on display at the fair. He accepted. The Canadian people, though, were upset with his plans to put these tiny, frail infants in a side show. So, the Canadian government stepped in and appointed guardians for the infants. These guardians, who had assisted in the births, were Dr. Dafoe, Judge J. A. Vallin, Minister David A. Cross, and Oliva Dionne, the father. The government also supplied a nurse.

On September 21, 1934, with a staff of twelve, the Dafoe Hospital was opened. This hospital, named after the Dionne quintuplets' doctor, was to be their new home for some time. It was here that Elzire named her new baby girls: *Marie, Emilie, Cecile, Yvonne,* and *Annette.*

The News Enterprise Association (also known as NEA) was chosen as the official company to photograph the Dionne Quints. And, Fred Davis, a photographer for the company, was selected to catch on film the little ones in everyday happenings. The NEA paid $25,000 a year for this right.

Chosen to represent the Dionne quintuplets in doll form was Madame Alexander and the Alexander Doll Company. This was indeed a boost for the young company, which had only been in business for a little over ten years. The first set of dolls manufactured showed the children in T-shirts with diapers, and were marked "ADCO" on the heads of the dolls. They were 7 1/2" tall, with painted eyes and molded hair, and the mark "Alexander" on their backs.

The first official set of Quint Dolls made wore bonnets, and white organdy dresses with bibs. They had wrist tags that were personalized. These were the first of several wrist tags manufactured. These dolls were marked "Dionne Alexander" on the head and "Alexander" on the body, and retailed for 79 cents.

From 1935 to 1936, many other sets were produced. FAO Schwarz had a special set made with a crib and baby bottles. At this time, many pieces of Dionne furniture could also be purchased, including a chair, a crib with mattress, and a white scooter with red wheels. These pieces were unmarked, but were believed to be produced by the SB Novelty Company out of New York.

The second set to follow was 10 1/2" tall, with sleep eyes and lashes. They wore knit booties and organdy dresses, and retailed from $1.69 to $1.95. This was a revolutionary set for the Alexander Doll Company, since it was the first time that the firm had used sleep eyes on dolls.

The next set was 18 1/2" tall, with a softcloth body and a crier. They were dressed in bonnets, and wore organdy dresses, moccasin slippers and socks. The clothes were marked with the name of each little girl. Retail price was $2.69.

Moving up in size, the next set produced dolls that were 23" tall, with a cry voice, molded hair, brown sleep eyes, and an open mouth with teeth. This was the first time that the open mouth was used on the Dionne Quint Dolls. They had cloth bodies, and were marked "Dionne Alexander." Retail price was $4.39.

Madame Alexander chose colors for each of the girls: blue for Marie, orchid for Emilie, green for Cecile, pink for Yvonne, and maize for Annette. And, on some of the dolls whose names were marked on them, Emilie's name was misspelled to read, "Emalie".

The momentum of the Quintuplet Dolls rose, with ads appearing in trade magazines like *Playthings* and *Toys and Novelty*. Stores like FAO Schwarz and Macy's ran wonderful store displays. Macy's even dressed the counter sales people as nurses. Dionne Quint Dolls were great sellers, and the stores wanted to capitalize on this. More wrist tags were produced with poems inside.

Soon, the girls were appearing everywhere. People could not get enough of them. Maud Faugel, a popular artist at the time, did a wonderful piece for the cover of *Woman's Home Companion*. The babies were 10 months old, and it was their first magazine cover. Many additional appearances followed, including three feature movies. The first was *The Country Doctor,* which depicted a fictional story of the Quints. This feature was released on March 6, 1936, and the girls were paid $50,000 for their participation. It took six filming sessions to complete the movie.

Madame Alexander, a master at marketing, thought of many ways to promote the dolls. The company put together a marketing campaign in which three sets of dolls and a bed set could be purchased at many Twentieth Century theaters. People could watch in excitement, seeing the little ones on the screen, and then, in the thrill of the moment, purchase the dolls to take home.

Set of Dionne Quints in original swing, $1,500 and up. Courtesy of Lynnae Ramsey.

In 1936, the first catalog produced by the Alexander Company was published, and it consisted entirely of Dionne Quintuplet Dolls in 7 1/2", 11", 15", 17", and 20" sizes. It also showed the Quints with human hair wigs. This is, indeed, a great item to have in your Dionne collection.

In the years 1936 and 1937, an 11" doll was produced that showed curly molded hair. You could see by the chubby legs on these dolls that the infants were now growing into little toddlers. This doll retailed for $1.85 to $2.75. Also available was the 17" version which retailed for $5.10, or an 18" soft body and composition doll that retailed for $4.50.

Madame Alexander took every chance to add another Dionne Quint to the collection. Making changes in the appearance gave people another reason to buy. And, many outfits were made for the dolls as well. The care and quality that went into these outfits was evident, right down to the lace trim on the panties. Madame Alexander was known for quality.

Ad for Lysol using the Dionne Quints. Courtesy of Nineteenth Century Imprints, Elisabeth Burdon.

From 1935 to 1938, the Dionne Quintuplet Dolls were made in various sizes, including 7-8", 10", 11-12", 14", 16", 20" and 23"-24".

Many pieces of furniture were also made, including:
- **A wooden table and chair set with the girls' names at each place setting.**
- **The Quint-O-Bile for the Quints to sit in and ride.**
- **A lawn swing**
- **A wooden swan**
- **A wooden duck rocking chair**
- **A merry-go-round**
- **Swings**
- **A Ferris wheel**
- **A seesaw**

Other items made were:
- **Wicker basket sets**
- **Specialty sets for individual stores**
- **Clothing which could be purchased separately**

One of the most rare items today is a bath set. Few were made, and even at the time, this piece drew much interest. This is an especially good find for today's collector.

Sales of the Quintuplet Dolls and accessories continued to grow through 1937. You could see the children everywhere, with manufacturers wanting to cash in on the Quints' popularity. There were many companies that used the Dionne babies for marketing. These companies included Beehive Golden Corn Syrup, Libby's Baby Food, Rexall, Lysol, Palmolive, Karo Syrup, Colgate, and others. And, many of these firms offered giveaways. Palmolive, for example, offered a set of Dionne quintuplet spoons, with the girls' images on the handles.

The Quints continued to be popular with the release of their second movie, *Reunion*. As predicted, this movie helped to sell more dolls and accessories. But, sales soared for more than just the Alexander Doll Company. Even fashion designers based some of their creations on clothes from the movie. Also, with thousands of visitors going to the Dionne Quints' birthplace and hospital, the Canadian Government estimated that 1/5 of all the tourism for the country was a direct result of the Dionne sisters.

In these years, three doll companies accounted for the majority of all doll sales in the United States. In first place was Ideal, with Shirley Temple; second place was Fleischaker and Baum, with Dy-Dee Baby; and, in third place, was Madame Alexander, with the Dionne Quints.

In 1937, the fifth wrist tag was made. With the quintuplets now growing older, they were no longer the tiny little infants that everyone watched so closely. The toddler stage was over, and the girls, going on four years old, were beginning to lose some of their public appeal. So, in 1938, Madame Alexander stopped making new models of the Quint Dolls—and began to shift her advertising away from the Quints and to her new favorite, Princess Elizabeth.

Ad campaigns were launched for the Princess Elizabeth Dolls, and ads for the Dionne Quintuplet Dolls slowed until they were almost nonexistent. The craze for the Dionne Quints was over. *Look* magazine put the girls on the cover for their fourth birthday. None of the major stores, though, created large displays as they had in the past. An era had ended. But for the five little girls born in that small house in Callendar, it was a life just beginning. They would, on occasion, make special appearances, but were eventually returned to live with their parents and other siblings.

When I think of the Dionne quintuplets, I think of those cute little infants with the big brown eyes and dark hair. They were so cute and adorable. The dolls that Madame Alexander produced are also in my thoughts. The work done on these dolls was, in my opinion, some of the finest—excellent detailing to both the features and the clothing. Adding those little extra items, like the wrist tags and nameplates, all made the Dionne Quintuplet Dolls special.

Set of 7" Dionne Quints in original bed, $1200 and up. Courtesy of Lynnae Ramsey.

PRICES OF VARIOUS DOLLS

7"-8"	$250
Matched set	$1,200-$1,500
10" baby	$325
11"-12" toddler	$375
14" toddler	$475
16" baby, cloth body	$475
20" toddler	$675
23"-24" baby, cloth body	$600

Individual pins used on many of the outfits: $75 each. values of the furniture pieces vary, and there are not enough comparisons to give accurate prices. As I mentioned before, they are worth what someone is willing to sell them for and what people are willing to pay. The most rare of the items is probably the bathtub, which I have only seen once at a doll show, for around $400.

Toddlers, all original of Yvonne and Annette. Courtesy of Pat Wood.

Group shot of the 11" Quint Toddlers. Courtesy of Lynnae Ramsey.

A set of the Dionne Quintuplets in all original clothing and chairs. Courtesy of Annette's Antique Dolls.

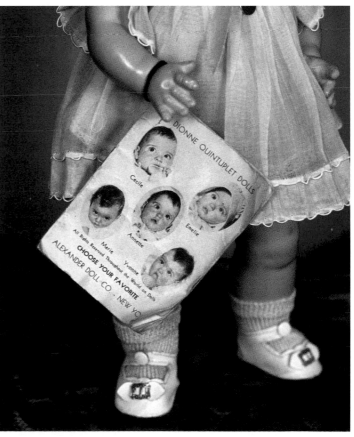

Close-up of wrist tag, Dionne Quint Toddler.

Nurse Doll
(Not Pictured)

Composition, $600-$750.

Named "Nurse Doll" because permission to use the name of the quintuplets' nurse was not obtained.

Doctor Doll (Dr. Dafoe)

Dr. Dafoe, 13", marked "Madame Alexander, New York" on clothing tag; "Created by Madame Alexander, New York" on one side of paper wrist tag; "An Alexander Product, Supreme Quality and Design" on flip side of tag. Composition head with character face; painted blue eyes; single stroke brows; painted upper lashes; closed smiling mouth; gray mohair wig; five-piece composition body. Dressed in tagged, white doctor outfit with matching cap; original socks and shoes. Here, he is shown with a 7 1/2" set of the Dionne Quintuplet babies in swing; $750-$1,000. (Dr. Dafoe sold through a McMaster's 1996 auction for $1,600, the Quints in Swing sold for $2,300).

Dionne Quint Toddler, all original, with wig, 11", $350-$375. Courtesy of Susan Killoran.

Quint, 11", molded hair, $350-$375. Courtesy of Susan Killoran.

Grouping of Dionne Quints, 7", straight and bent-legged babies. Blue outfits, original. If all original, $250 each. Susan Killoran Collection.

Dionne Quint Toddler, 11", molded hair, $250-$375. Susan Killoran Collection.

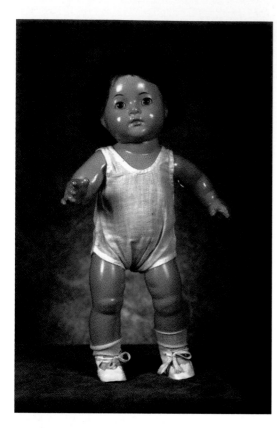

Dionne Quint, all composition, closed mouth. Courtesy of Susan Killoran.

Group shot of different sizes and ages of the Dionne Quints. Courtesy of Susan Killoran.

Dionne Quint, all composition, opened mouth. Courtesy of Susan Killoran.

Dionne Girl, 19", all composition with wig, redressed. Courtesy of Susan Killoran.

Dionne Quints, 7 1/2", all original and tagged; with wigs, shoes, bonnets, pins, extra sun-suits with bonnets, $1,500. Courtesy of Susan Killoran.

Quintuplet bowls with two spoons. Courtesy of Susan Killoran.

Alexander Quint. Courtesy of Sunnie Newell.

include many things—including rugs, clocks, handker-
chiefs, and radios.

*Ad for Colgate dental cream with the Toddler
Quints and Dr. Dafoe. Courtesy of Susan Killoran.*

*Advertisement for Palmolive soap with two of the five spoons. Send-away
offer to receive souvenir Quint teaspoons. Courtesy of Susan Killoran.*

THE DIONNE QUINTUPLETS

BELLINGHAM BUILDERS SUPPLY CO.
COAL

Tru-Mix Concrete
Brick, Lime and Plaster
Sand, Gravel and Cement
Concrete Products

Coke and Carbon Briquets
Store and Burner Oil
Office and Display Room: "C" and Chestnut St.
Dock and Bunkers: "C" and Maple St.
Phones 78 and 79

Du Pont Powder
Roofing and Roof Coatings
Plaster, Lath and Wallboard
Coal Stokers

YVONNE   MARIE   ANNETTE   EMILIE   CECILE

*Calendar top showing the young Dionne Quints.
Courtesy of Susan Killoran.*

Liberty

GERMANY'S SECRET PLANS FOR INVADING ENGLAN
The Inside Story by Wythe Williams

*Another magazine cover graced with the
Quints' image. This one is Liberty 1941.
Courtesy of Susan Killoran.*

Photo of the Quintuplets as young adults. Courtesy of Susan Killoran.

Alexander Boy Blue, 7", with Carmen, 7". Composition heads with painted blue eyes; clothing is all original. Boy Blue sold for $305 and Carmen for $105 at a 1996 McMaster's Doll Auction. Courtesy of McMaster's Doll Auction.

Bride Doll, 23", all original, $350-$400. Author's Collection.

Alice in Wonderland, all original, 1947; 14" (shown), $350-$450; 18", $450-$550. Courtesy of Pat Wood.

Alice in Wonderland, 18"; marked "Madame Alexander" on back of head; "Alice in Wonderland,' by Madame Alexander, N.Y., All Rights Reserved" on dress tag; "Madame Alexander, Alice in Wonderland" on label on box. Composition head, hazel sleep eyes, real lashes, eye shadow, painted lower lashes, closed mouth, original human hair wig, five-piece composition body. Dressed in original blue/white print dress and white organdy pinafore; shown here with an all original Sonja Henie, 17". (See page 150.) Courtesy of McMaster's Doll Auctions.

BABY MCGUFFEY & BUTCH
*Left is Baby McGuffey, marked
"Madame Alexander" on back of head,
"NY, All Rights Reserved" on dress tag.
Composition head, brown sleep eyes, real
lashes, painted lower lashes, closed
mouth, original mohair wig, cloth body,
and composition hands and lower legs.
Dressed in pink tagged dress, white eyelet
pinafore, matching bonnet, long stockings, snap shoes. Shown here with Butch
on right. Courtesy of McMaster's Doll
Auctions. 11", $150-$250.*

BETTY

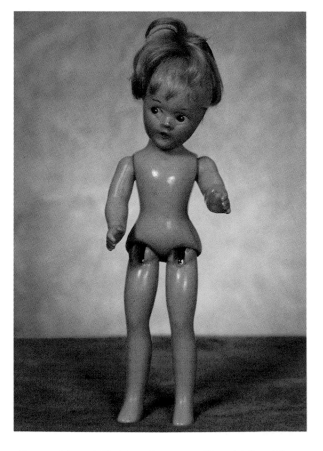

Composition, 10", jointed at arms, hinged-jointed legs.

Little Betty Bride, made in 1936, $150-$225. Courtesy of Pat Wood.

BRIDESMAID—1940

18", all original, with brown sleep eyes, original set mohair wig; 14", $275-$325; 18", $375-$475. Courtesy of Pat Wood.

FLORA MCFLIMSEY

Left is Flora McFlimsey, marked "13" on back; "Flora McFlimsey of Madison Square, Madame Alexander, NY USA, All Rights Reserved" on dress tag; "Flora McFlimsey, An Alexander Product" on one side of paper wrist tag; "Created by Madame Alexander, New York" on flip side of paper wrist tag; 13", composition head, blue sleep eyes, real lashes, painted lower lashes, opened mouth with four teeth, freckles on bridge of nose, red human hair wig, five-piece composition body. She is wearing an original tagged green dress, white pinafore with green ribbon trim, white socks and brown high snap shoes, green straw bonnet; $500-$800. Shown here with Arranbee Nancy, $300-$350. Courtesy of McMaster's Doll Auctions.

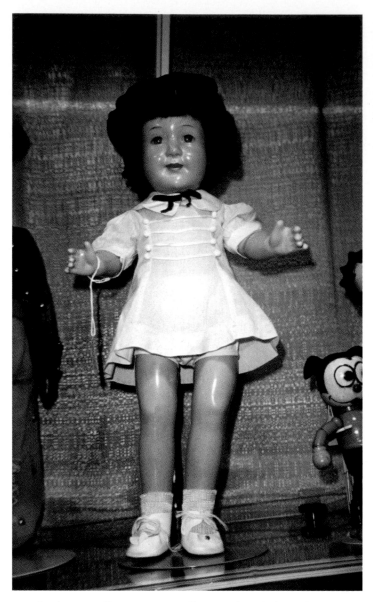

Made in 1937, all composition, all original, 15", $750-$900. Courtesy of Annette's Antique Dolls.

Marked "Jane Withers" on script pin; "Jane Withers, All Rights Reserved, Madame Alexander, NY" on dress tag. Composition head with character face, blue sleep eyes with real lashes, feathered brows, painted lower lashes, opened mouth with four upper teeth, original brunette wig in original set, five-piece composition body. Dressed in original tagged dress with pink and blue flowers, one-piece underwear combination, original shoes and socks, pink hat; 15", $900-$1,000. Courtesy of McMaster's Doll Auctions.

Jeannie Walker, 14" & 19". Courtesy of Pat Wood.

Jeannie Walker, 14", all original. Courtesy of Pat Wood.

Left is a 13" Jeannie Walker, marked "Alexander, Pat No.2171281" on back; "Jeannie Walker, Madame Alexander, NY USA, All Rights Reserved" on dress tag; "Madame Alexander, 3715, Alexander Doll Company, New York, NY, Jeannie Walker" stamped on box's end label. Composition head, brown sleep eyes, real lashes, gray eye shadow, painted lower lashes, closed mouth, mohair wig, composition body with wooden walking mechanism at lower torso. Dressed in original, tagged, red, plaid dress with attached half slip, navy blue felt hat. Right is a 14" Margaret O'Brien Doll marked "Madame Alexander, New York USA," on dress tag; "Margaret O'Brien, All Rights Reserved" on one side of foil wrist tag; "A Madame Alexander Doll" on flip side of tag, "Madame Alexander, Style 3331, Alexander Doll Company, New York, NY, Margaret O'Brien" stamped on end of box. Composition character head, blue sleep eyes, real lashes, single stroke brow, painted lower lashes, closed mouth, original mohair wig, five-piece composition child body. Dressed in tagged aqua dress with white nylon eyelet trim, imitation straw hat, $600-$900. Shown with Margaret O'Brien (See "Margaret O'Brien" for description). Courtesy of McMaster's Doll Auctions.

MADELEINE

Madeleine, 17", composition with sleep eyes, original human hair wig with original clothing, $500-$600. Shown with 14" Alexander Bridesmaid. Courtesy of McMaster's Doll Auctions.

MARGARET O'BRIEN

Made in 1946; all composition with sleep eyes and braided wig; usually found with brown hair, but made with red hair as well; 14", $500-$600; 18", $650-$750.

Margaret O'Brien, 18" with red hair and blue eyes. Courtesy of Lynnae Ramsey.

Margaret O'Brien, 14" with brown hair and brown eyes. Courtesy of Lynnae Ramsey.

MARCELLA

Marcella, 6", composition with sleep eyes, original outfit, $150-$200. Courtesy of McMaster's Doll Auctions.

Margaret O'Brien, 14"; marked "Madame Alexander, New York USA," on dress tag; "Margaret O'Brien, All Rights Reserved" on one side of foil wrist tag; "A Madame Alexander Doll" on flip side of tag, "Madame Alexander Style 3331, Alexander Doll Company, New York, NY, stamped Margaret O'Brien" on box's label. Composition character head, blue sleep eyes, real lashes, painted lower lashes, closed mouth, original mohair wig, five- piece composition body. Dressed in tagged aqua dress with white nylon eyelet trim, imitation straw hat. Courtesy of McMaster's Doll Auctions.

MCGUFFEY ANA

Made in 1937; all composition, jointed at neck, shoulders, and hips; mohair or human hair wig; sleep eyes, opened mouth; 13", $375-$425; 18"-20", $450-$525; 24", $600-$650.

Beautiful McGuffey Ana in original tagged dress with paper tag. Courtesy of Pat Wood.

McGuffey Ana, 13", all original, with replaced shoes. Courtesy of Lynnae Ramsey.

All original McGuffey Ana, 19". Courtesy of McMaster's Doll Auction.

Same as above, with close-up of tag marked "School House, I am McGuffey Ana."

MISS AMERICA

Made in 1939, 14", $550-$675. Rare doll to find. All
original, except flag. Courtesy of Pat Wood.

PRINCE CHARMING

Alexander Boy, redressed as Prince Charming, all compo-
sition, beautiful sleep eyes, yarn-type hair, $500-$600.
Courtesy of Lynnae Ramsey.

PRINCESS ELIZABETH

1937, all composition; sleep eyes; mohair or human
hair wig; jointed at neck, shoulders, and hips; marked
"PRINCESS ELIZABETH ALEXANDER DOLL
CO," 16"-18", $350-$425; 22"-24", $500-$600; 27",
$675-$750.

Princess Elizabeth, 15", all original, $350-$400. Courtesy of
Susan Killoran.

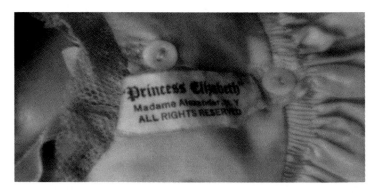

Dress tag from a Princess Elizabeth Doll.

All original, beautiful example. Courtesy of Sharron's Dolls.

Princess Elizabeth, 14", made in 1942, all original, marked on back of head with circle with an X. Courtesy of Pat Wood.

Left: Princess Elizabeth, 16", with box. Marked "Princess Elizabeth, Alexander Doll" on back of head; "Princess Elizabeth, Madame Alexander, NY, USA, All Rights Reserved" on tag on dress; "Princess Elizabeth, 3887 T, Madame Alexander" on label on box. Composition head, blue sleep eyes, real lashes, painted lower lashes, opened mouth with four teeth, original human hair wig, five-piece composition body. Dressed in peach taffeta dress with original tiara. Courtesy of McMaster's Doll Auctions.

Far left: Princess Elizabeth, all original, 24". Courtesy of Lynnae Ramsey.

SCARLETT O'HARA—1937

Black hair, composition with sleep eyes, jointed at arms and legs, all original; 11", $400-$500; 14", $600-$700; 18", $800-$900; 21", $1,000 and up.

Scarlett. Courtesy of Sharron's Dolls.

Wonderful Scarlett O'Hara, all original, 11", with original wrist tag and original box, $500-$800. Courtesy of McMaster's Doll Auction.

Scarlett, 14", in original Southern Belle outfit, tagged coat and dress, made in 1942, $600 and up. Courtesy of Pat Wood.

Scarlett, 14", in rare outfit, all original with original box, $650 and up. Courtesy of Pat Wood.

Rare Scarlett O'Hara advertising doll. Advertising "SCARLETT, A Fantastic New Shade From the Old South in NO MEND Silk Stockings." All original, with advertising and paper hang tags, $1,000 and up. Courtesy of McCarthy & Associates.

Close-up of tags.

SNOW WHITE

This undressed Snow White shows the position of the legs and arms; she has black hair, sleep eyes, and closed painted mouth; her coloring is much whiter than other composition dolls of her time; $250 undressed, $500-$600 with original outfit. This doll was made using the Princess Elizabeth mold.

SONJA HENIE—1939

Composition, jointed at neck, hips, and shoulders; smiling opened mouth with teeth; sleep eyes; human hair or mohair wig; original clothes; was also made on the Wendy Ann body with a swivel waist, marked "MADAME ALEXANDER—SONJA HENIE" on back of neck. Dress was marked "Sonja Henie."

Sonja Henie was born on April 8, 1912, in Oslo, Norway. She grew up happy and well-to-do, with the Henie family wealth going back four generations. She was two years old when World War I began, and the family moved to a summer home in Denmark. She had a talent for the drums and piano, but ice skating became her passion. When she was just five years old, her brother Lief clipped her first pair of skates to her shoes. She would chase him all around as he played hockey. Also at five, she entered her first contest for children and won first prize, a pearl-handled silver paper cutter. So started the career of Sonja Henie.

In her years of skating, she would become the greatest female skater of all time, winning an unprecedented three Olympics. The first Olympics she entered was in 1924 in Chamonix. She placed eighth. In 1928, she wowed the hearts of all by winning the Olympics in St. Moritz. She went on to finish first again in 1932 in Lake Placid, and in 1936 in Garmisch-Partenkirchen. Three Olympic Gold medals! But this was not her only accomplishment. Sonja also won the World Championship Figure Skating finals for ten consecutive years. This was an unbelievable record and is still unbeaten. These championships occurred during the years 1927 to 1936, three years before Madame Alexander put this wonder-on-ice into doll form.

Photo of Sonja Henie.

Sonja Henie, all original, 14", $350-$425; 17", $425-$500; 18", $600-$750; 21", $800 and up. Author's Collection.

Two award-winning Sonja Henie Dolls, all original. Courtesy of Pat Wood.

Sonja Henie, marked "Genuine 'Sonja Henie' Doll, Madame Alexander, NY USA" on tag on clothing; "Sonja Henie, Madame Alexander 3424R" on box's end label. Composition head with character face, brown sleep eyes, real lashes, painted lower lashes, opened smiling mouth with six teeth, dimples, human hair wig, five-piece composition body. Dressed in tagged red corduroy jacket with silver buttons, matching fur-trimmed hat, blue pants with attached white skis, ski poles, 17", $600-$1,000. Courtesy of McMaster's Doll Auctions.

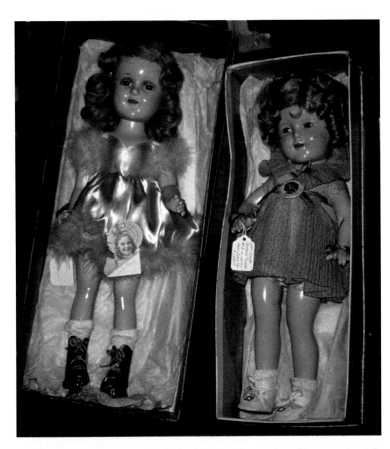

Sonja Henie with mint Ideal Shirley Temple nearby; all original, with original boxes. Courtesy of Sharron's Dolls.

All original Sonja Henie, with case and extra clothing. Courtesy of Sharron's Dolls.

Another 21" doll wearing a Toni dress. Courtesy of Susan Newell.

Drene advertisement from 1939 with 14" Sonja Henie in original outfit, $350-$425. Courtesy of Susan Killoran.

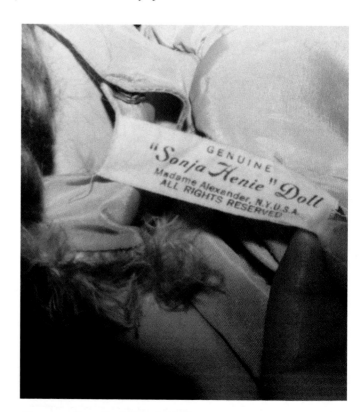

Dress tag from Sonja Henie Doll.

Sonja Henie, 14", 1939, original outfit, $350-$425. Courtesy of Susan Killoran.

Sonja Henie, 21", $800 and up. In this redressed outfit, $450. Courtesy of Susan Killoran.

Advertisement for Drene shampoo, showing Sonja Henie. Courtesy of Susan Killoran.

SPANISH & SCOTTISH GIRLS

Marked "Wendy-Ann, Mme Alexander, New York" on back of both dolls. Both dolls, 9", have composition heads, painted blue eyes to side, closed mouths, original mohair wigs, five-piece composition bodies. Both dolls are dressed in original tagged clothing; $200-$300 for pair. Courtesy of McMaster's Doll Auctions.

SPECIAL GIRL

Composition arms, legs, and head with cloth body, 1942-1946, 22", $400-$500. Courtesy of Pat Wood.

ALEXANDER DOLLS NOT INCLUDED

CYNTHIA
(See Chapter 4, "Black Composition Dolls")

DISNEY MARIONETTES
Composition and strings, 10"-12", $350.

TOPSY TURVY 1936
Composition, 7 1/2", $175.

TONY SARG MARIONETTES

Composition and strings; character faces; 10"-12", $150 each.

(For other Tony Sarg Dolls, see Chapter 4, "Black Composition Dolls")

Two Tony Sarg Marionettes with Playbook.

Above Left: Tony Sarg Playbook showing that the Marionettes were manufactured exclusively by Madame Alexander, New York, USA.

Above Right: Back cover of the Tony Sarg Playbook, marked "ALEXANDER DOLL COMPANY New York, All rights reserved."

Rare Schoenhut Soldier Boy, all original with leather outfit, made in 1911. Courtesy of Pat Wood.

CHAPTER ELEVEN
SCHOENHUT DOLLS & TOYS

The Schoenhut Company was founded by Albert Schoenhut. Born in Germany in 1849, and in the third generation of toy makers in the Schoenhut family, he moved to Philadelphia and founded his own company in 1872, and began to manufacture toy pianos. By the 1890s, he was producing store displays, many of which were mechanical. At this time, he also produced fully wood-jointed figures; these figures fueled growth of the doll designs that would captivate children everywhere.

In February 1902, a German citizen named Fritz Meinecke, who was living in Philadelphia, applied for a patent for a toy animal. He assigned the patent to Albert Schoenhut. Fritz Meinecke then sold the patent to Albert, and that was the start of the Humpty Dumpty Circus. The tremendous success of the Circus pieces caused great growth within the Schoenhut Company. The selection of pieces for one's collection grew, and so did the sales.

At the beginning of 1909, Theodore Roosevelt sailed to Africa, and by the middle of that year, Albert Schoenhut had designed pieces entitled "Teddy's Adventures in Africa." The animals designed to go with this set were later added to the circus line. In 1911, Albert applied for, and received, a patent for a spring-jointed doll figure. These figures named "Teddy," and members of his American hunting party, became popular pieces as well, and further increased the interest of the spring-jointed dolls (which would begin to be man-

ufactured in 1911). The new spring-jointed dolls were manufactured in a series, including:

  100 series: Carved Hair Girls
  200 series: Carved Hair Boys
  300 series: Wigged Girls
  400 series: Wigged Boys

Other designs would follow, and his famous designs would be perfected straight into the 1920s.

Felix the Cat, copyright by Pat Sullivan, wood-jointed with segmented tail and leather ears; 4", $175-$200; 6", $250-$375; 8", $350-$450. Author's Collection.

Grouping of Schoenhut characters: Boy, 11", $600 and up; Baby with composition body, 10", $500; Girl with wig, all original, $600 and up. Courtesy of Lynnae Ramsey.

Dolly Face Schoenhut on left, marked "Schoenhut Doll, Pat. Jan 17th 1911, USA" on oval label on back, 14", $100-$300; Schoenhut Nature Baby on right, marked "Schoenhut, c" on back of head, 12", $100-$300. Courtesy of McMaster's Doll Auctions.

Girl, all wood, spring-jointed body, wooden head, mohair wig, $600-$700. Author's Collection.

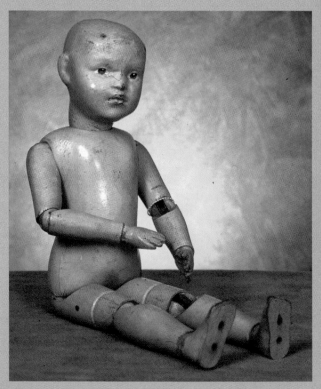

Boy, all wood, spring-jointed body, wooden head, missing wig, $500. Author's Collection.

Group shot of wonderful Schoenhut Dolls
with Shirley looking on. Courtesy of
Cobb's Doll Auction.

Barney and Spark Plug, all original, $400-$500. Courtesy of Annette's Antique Dolls.

Wood-jointed figure of Barney Google; Barney is wearing a top hat, cloth jacket, and checked brown trousers, with original Schoenhut pin, 7 3/4", $400-$500. Courtesy of Christie's Images.

A Schoenhut boxed set of Maggie and Jiggs, wood-jointed figures, circa 1925. Both figures have hand-painted features, and are cloth-dressed in period clothing; Maggie, 10"; Jiggs, 8"; $1,000-$1,500. Sold at a Christie's Auction for $2,350. Courtesy of Christie's Images.

Maggie & Jiggs—Maggie stands at 9", and Jiggs at 7"; $400-$600 for pair. Courtesy of Carl Kludt.

A Schoenhut Roly Poly of Little Nemo's "Dr. Pimm," hand-painted composition; the Doctor is wearing a very tall top hat and wire glasses, 11 1/2". This piece was estimated at $500-$700 at Christie's Character Auction, but sold for $3,960. Courtesy of Christie's Images.

Schoenhut "Boob McNutt" on left, dressed in flowered baggy trousers with jointed arms and legs, hand-painted face, 9", $1,000 and up. On right is "Barney Google," a wood-jointed comic character, c. 1922, with hand-painted face, original clothes, and jointed arms and legs, stamp on right foot with Schoenhut pin, 8 1/2", $500. Courtesy of Christie's Images. (Center item is a cast-iron Barney Google Hood Ornament in a wooden frame, $300-$500.)

All original Schoenhut African Chief, from the Teddy Roosevelt set, $1,000-$1,500. Courtesy of James & Judy Sneed.

Schoenhut Goat with Ringmaster. Goat, $150-$250; Ringmaster, $100-$150. Courtesy of James & Judy Sneed.

All original Schoenhut "Negro Dude," $350-$450. Courtesy of James & Judy Sneed.

Close-up of Schoenhut Leopard. Courtesy of James & Judy Sneed.

Schoenhut Arabian Camel, $250-$350. Courtesy of James & Judy Sneed.

Schoenhut Alligator, $400-$500. Courtesy of James & Judy Sneed.

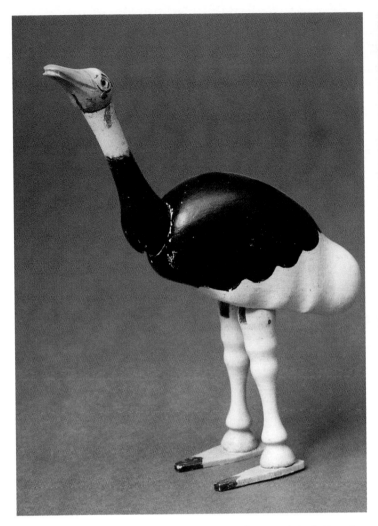

Schoenhut Ostrich, $250-$350. Courtesy of James & Judy Sneed.

Schoenhut Giraffe, $150-$250. Courtesy of James & Judy Sneed.

Schoenhut Brown and White Bears, $275-$350. Courtesy of James & Judy Sneed.

Schoenhut Zebra, $275-$325. Courtesy of James & Judy Sneed.

Schoenhut Clown in original outfit, $100-$200.
Courtesy of James & Judy Sneed.

Schoenhut Goat with Clown. Goat, $150-$250; Clown, $100-$200. Courtesy of James & Judy Sneed.

Grouping of Schoenhut Clowns in original outfits. Author's Collection.

Schoenhut Clowns, all original, $150-$300. Courtesy of James & Judy Sneed.

Schoenhut Lady Acrobat with Leopards. Leopards, $250-$350 each. Courtesy of James & Judy Sneed.

Schoenhut Lady Circus Riders with three hair colors, $250-$400 each. Courtesy of James & Judy Sneed.

Schoenhut Elephants with Ringmaster. Elephants, $100-$150. Courtesy of James & Judy Sneed.

Schoenhut Hippos with Lady Circus Rider. Hippos, $200-$300. Courtesy of James & Judy Sneed.

Schoenhut Lady Acrobat with stands, jointed to move for flexibility; $250-$350. Courtesy of James & Judy Sneed.

Schoenhut Hobos, $150-$250. Courtesy of James & Judy Sneed.

All original Schoenhut Hobo. Courtesy of James & Judy Sneed.

Schoenhut Lady Circus Rider with Elephants. Courtesy of James & Judy Sneed.

Above & top left: Group shots of the Humpty Dumpty Circus.

Schoenhut's Humpty Dumpty Circus, marked "Schoenhut's Humpty Dumpty Circus, The Greatest Toys on Earth" on top of lid; "Humpty Dumpty Toys, Seneca Falls, New York, Set 2" on end of lid; "Humpty Dumpty Toys" in circle stamped on bottom of chair. Set includes clown, 7", with painted features; painted-eye donkey, 7", with leather ears and rope tail; white chairs for clowns, 4 1/2"; red, white, and blue barrel, 2 1/2", $300-$400. Courtesy of McMaster's Doll Auctions.

Schoenhut Lion with box, $275-$325, add $50 for box. Courtesy of James & Judy Sneed.

Schoenhut White Horse, with original box. With box, $250 and up; without box, $150-$200. Courtesy of James & Judy Sneed.

Schoenhut Group Shot of Circus Tent and Accessories, 35 1/2" long by 24 1/2" wide, $2,000-$2,500. Courtesy of Cobb's Doll Auctions.

A Ted Toy Teddy Soldier, blue body with painted features, shoe string-type arms and legs on green base with pull string, $75-$125. Courtesy of James & Judy Sneed.

CHAPTER TWELVE
TED TOYLER INC.

According to James and Judy Sneed, collectors of Toyler Toys, Ted Toyler Inc. of New Bedford, Massachusetts, operated from about 1925 until 1930. By 1929, they had merged with the International Toy Company. Earlier toys are marked "Ted Toyler," while later ones carried the International Toy Company logo. Over 30 models were made, including pull toys, dolls, doll houses, and construction sets. E. V. Babbit seems to have been the driving force behind the Ted Toyler Company. Toy Tinkers—very popular at the time—were very similar to, and were sold in competition against, TedToy-lers. For comparison purposes, I have included several of the Toy Tinkers in this chapter.

Watch them march! TedToy-lers Soldiers, a Ted Toy, all wood with wood-jointed arms; painted, smiling face; metal gun; $100-$150. Courtesy of James & Judy Sneed.

TINKER TOYS

Look for the RED TINKER MEN on the carton—it's your assurance of a genuine Tinker Toy.

PONY TINKER
is the horsie's name. The rider posts up and down in graceful fashion whenever horsie is pulled along the floor or walk.

LANKY TINKER
tall, thin and handsome, is so strong that no amount of tumbling around or rough abuse can hurt him.

DRAG-ON TINKER
so named because as you drag him on, he wiggles and squirms—like the Dragons of old. He cannot be hurt.

TINKER TOYS are the ideal toys for children. They are sturdily made to resist breakage—no sharp corners—and are painted with fast, harmless colors. Made for play, education and to provide mothers more leisure. Twenty-five toys to choose from. All popularly priced. Can be had at all dealers where good toys are sold.

The Toy Tinkers-Inc.
EVANSTON—ILLINOIS

—and Such A Happy Dream!

SHE dreams that with Old Mother Goose she has just arrived in Tinker Toy Land, riding a Choo Choo Tinker. Hurrah, there's going to be a Tinker Toy Circus! Pony Tinker leads the parade with his rider that bounces up and down. Clown Tinker does all sorts of funny things that make Belle and Tom Tinker clap their hands with joy. Then come Siren Tinker, with Follow-Me Tinker, Drag-on Tinker and Whirly Tinker with the funny twins.

Oh, it's heaps of fun in Tinker Toy Land!

Tinker Toys are sold at the better stores, in Toy and Infant Departments.

From the Shops of
The TOY TINKERS, Inc.
EVANSTON, ILL.

Oh—Mother—Look!
TINKER TOYS!

CHILDREN everywhere know these fascinating, colorful toys. Mothers everywhere recognize them as safe playmates for their children. Ask to see Tinker Toys at any toy store or toy department. Sold everywhere.

The TOY TINKERS, Inc.
EVANSTON, ILLINOIS

Run! TOM TINKER Run!!

WHIST! Halloween! Witches and black cats everywhere! "Whoa," Pony Tinker cries to Tom, "Jump on my back and we'll race through the still black night."

There's fun for the children in every Tinker Toy. Every merchant who carries toys has TINKER TOYS.

The TOY TINKERS, Inc.
EVANSTON, ILLINOIS.

Above: The Toy Tinkers, Inc., Child Life magazine ad. Courtesy of Vicki Lane.

Left: "Run! Tom Tinker Run!" states this Child Life magazine ad with Pony Tinker and Tom Tinker. Courtesy of Vicki Lane.

Above: From the pages of Child Life magazine, this ad shows Pony Tinker, Lanky Tinker and Drag-On Tinker. Wooden toys were very popular during the 1920s and 1930s. Courtesy of Vicki Lane.

Left: The Toy Tinker ad for wooden crib type toys. This also pictures a Toy Tinker pull train. Crib toys, $25-$50; Train, $75-$100. Courtesy of Vicki Lane.

Tinker Toys were very similar to the TedToy-lers.

Above: TedToy-lers Soldiers, a Ted Toy, marked "Teddy Soldier, Built by Ted Toy-lers Inc. at New Bedford, Mass. USA." Brightly colored soldiers on a green base with pull string. Original box, $125-$200. Courtesy of James & Judy Sneed.

Right: Hop on the Ted Toy Express! This little guy is off with his white horses on a green base, $100-$150. Courtesy of James & Judy Sneed.

*TedToy-lers, a Ted Toy, Teddy Soldier with box, $100-$150.
Courtesy of James & Judy Sneed.*

*Ted Toy with regular-sized Galloping Jockey shows the size of the
Giant Soldier at 15" high, $100-$150. Courtesy of James & Judy
Sneed. (These pieces came in both regular and giant size.)*

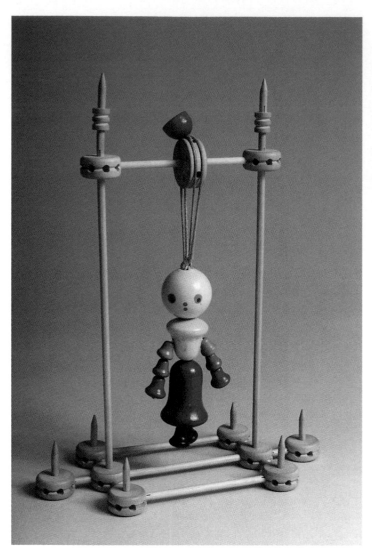

Toy Tinker, $50-$75. Courtesy of James & Judy Sneed.

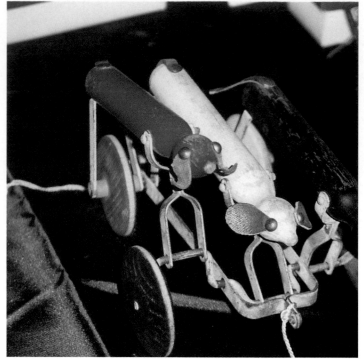

Tinker Dogs Pull Toy, in black, white, and red; wood on metal base; leather ears, metal eyes; $75-$100. Courtesy of Golden Arrow Toy Co.

Above: Ted Toy from the Giant Series, a Galloping Jockey. This oversized toy is cute as can be and built to stand the rigors of young hands, $100-$150. Courtesy of James & Judy Sneed.

Right: The TedToy-lers of New Bedford, Massachusetts, "Giant Galloping Jockey," bright multicolored clown sits upon a yellow and black horse with red hoofs and stand. He sits upon a green base with pull string, $100-$150. Courtesy of James & Judy Sneed.

Right: The Toy Tinkers Inc. "Tinker Mule," made around 1928 in Evanston, Illinois; shows a black man holding on to a donkey's tail. It moves up and down when pulled by metal and wood base. Hat is marked "The Toy Tinker Inc., Evanston, Ill., USA," $150-$250. Courtesy of James & Judy Sneed.

Patsy-Type, 13", $125-$150.
Courtesy of Susan Killoran.

CHAPTER THIRTEEN
UNMARKED DOLLS

Unmarked dolls and toys cover a wide variety of items. All dolls and toys were made by someone, somewhere; the only problem is that many of these companies, for one reason or another, did not mark their creations with the company's identifying marks. Some of these items can be easily identified, while others will keep you searching for months for their origin. Perhaps this chapter will help you to solve one of your mysteries. The prices on unmarked dolls and toys are generally lower than marked ones.

Left: A Foxy Grandpa Roly-Poly, painted composition with swivel head and round body, wearing an orange coat and tie with hands at belly, 10 1/4", $300-$400. Courtesy of Christie's Images.

Above: Boy, 20", great molded hair, unmarked, composition with tin eyes, opened mouth, $150-$175. Courtesy of Susan Killoran.

Left: Tin-eyed composition Toddler, molded hair, 17" tall, $75-$125. Courtesy of Susan Killoran.

Above: Tin-eyed Baby Girl, molded hair, $75-$125. Courtesy of Susan Killoran.

Bottom Left: Tin-eyed Baby with molded hair and curved legs, sleep eyes, $75-$100. Courtesy of Susan Killoran.

Bottom Right: Another tin sleep-eyed composition Little Girl; composition head, arms, and legs; shoulder plate connecting cloth body; opened mouth; 20", $150-$225. Courtesy of Susan Killoran.

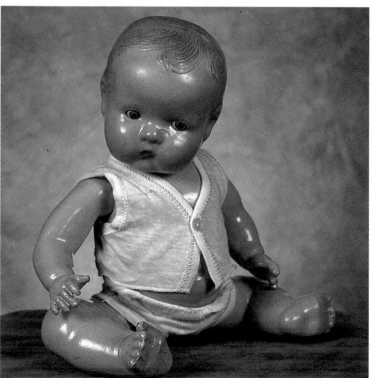

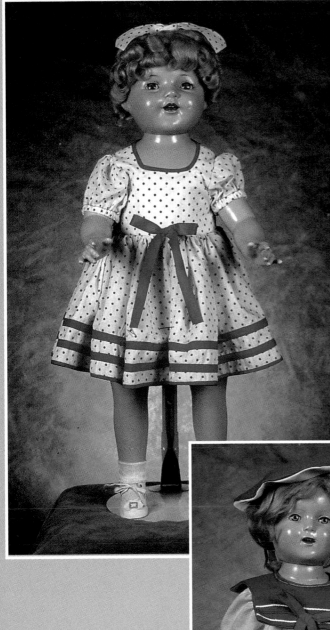

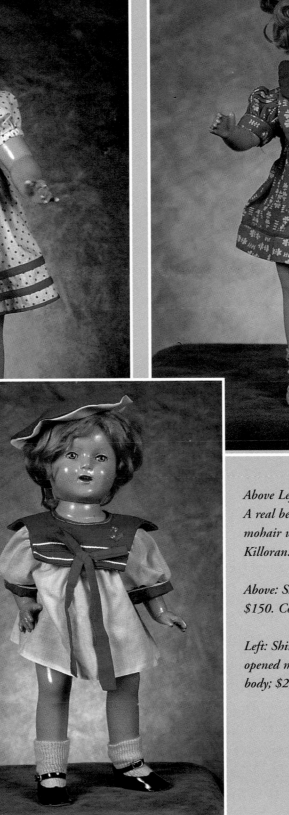

Above Left: Unmarked Shirley Temple look-alike. A real beauty at 28" tall. All composition with mohair wig, $300-$400. Courtesy of Susan Killoran.

Above: Shirley Temple look-alike, 14", $125-$150. Courtesy of Susan Killoran.

Left: Shirley Temple look-alike, 20", tin eyes, opened mouth; composition arms, legs, head, and body; $250-$300. Courtesy of Susan Killoran.

Top Left: *Tin-eyed Girl with sleep eyes, opened mouth, original braided wig, $125-$150. Courtesy of Susan Killoran.*

Top Right: *This composition Girl has an opened mouth, sleep eyes, and has that "Shirley" appearance, 25", $225-$275. Courtesy of Susan Killoran.*

Beautiful 27" unmarked Girl Doll, opened mouth with teeth, brown sleep eyes, mohair wig, $150-$200. Courtesy of Susan Killoran.

Composition Girl, 12", cloth body, sleep eyes, mohair wig $175-$200. Author's Collection.

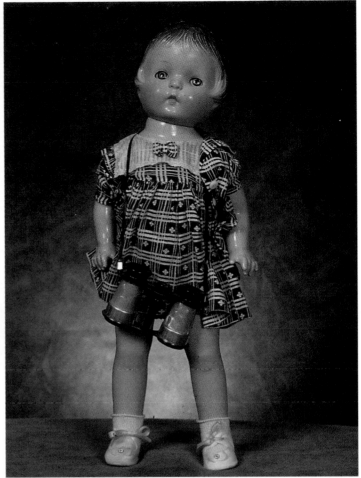

Composition Patsy-type doll, tin sleep eyes, 18", $175-$200. Author's Collection.

Clothes Pin Dolls, 4", all wood, $25-$50 each. Courtesy of Sunnie Newell.

Jointed composition Elephant, unmarked, curved body with segmented trunk, unusual piece, $75-$125. Author's Collection.

Far Left: Unmarked composition little Toddler Baby, sleep eyes, closed mouth, mohair wig. Sitting with friend, $150-$175. Author's Collection.

Left: Composition Baby with cloth body, flirty eyes, molded hair, 21", $150-$200. Author's Collection.

Girl Doll, tin eyes, stuffed cloth body, 13", $85-$135. Author's Collection.

Shirley Temple look-alike. All composition, opened mouth, 26", $200-$300. Author's Collection.

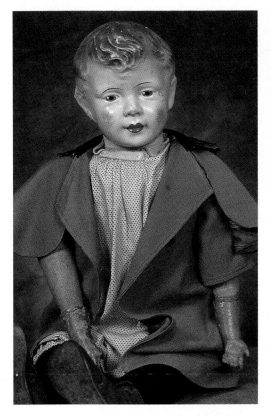

Above Left: Unmarked Boy Doll, cloth arms and body, straw stuffed legs, with composition face and hands, unusual size for a boy doll at 32", $275-$350. Author's Collection.

Above: Boy Doll, tin sleep eyes, cloth body, 23", $150-$175. Author's Collection.

Above Right: Composition Patsy look-alike, 8", painted features, all original, $90-$125. Author's Collection.

Left: Mae West-type Doll, cloth body, 18", sleep eyes; composition head, arms, and legs; $175-$200. Author's Collection.

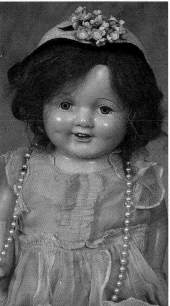

Beautiful Girl Doll with cloth body, sleep tin eyes, 23"; composition arms, legs, and head; $225-$275. Author's Collection.

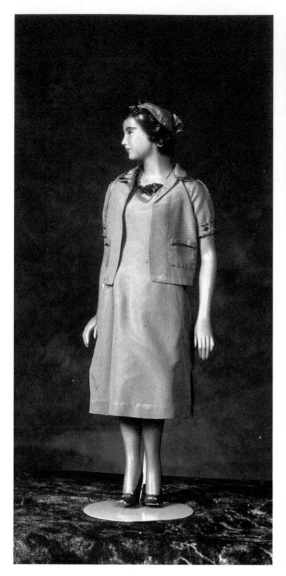

Far Left: Unmarked Lady Doll, used as a model for sewing classes, all composition, painted features, 22", $150-$300. Courtesy of Sunnie Newell.

Left: This wonderful Shirley Temple look-alike, 29", was found at a local secondhand store for $35 in 1990; worth $550-$750. What a find! She has no markings. Courtesy of Sunnie Newell.

Right: An excellent example of an Uncle Sam Doll. Uncle Sam dolls are rare and not usually found in such nice condition; cloth body with composition hands and feet, molded head, $550-$750. Courtesy of Irene's Archives.

Far Right: Unmarked Nurse Doll, 8", composition with painted features, jointed at shoulders, all original, $75. Courtesy of Sunnie Newell.

Trudy, the Three-Faced Doll; made in 1946; composition head with cloth body, 14", $225-$275. Turn knob on top of head to see her different expressions. Author's Collection.

Googly-Eyed Dolls. These dolls were made with fabric bodies, composition heads, and inset eyes that moved back and forth when the doll was moved. This photo includes a 17" doll with no feet, and a 16" doll with wooden feet. They came in a variety of sizes and were marketed through Sears in 1945; $100-$150. Courtesy of Sunnie Newell (See Chapter 4, "Black Composition Dolls.")

Boy Doll, painted eyes, composition with straw body and legs, 18", $175-$250. Courtesy of Lynnae Ramsey.

Composition Little Girl with painted features, molded hair, 7", $75, from Japan.

Right: 14", all composition Girl Doll; jointed at shoulders, arms, and legs; new wig, sleep eyes, painted mouth. Cute doll, but I've not been able to find out much about her; $100-$150.

Two unmarked dolls, composition with painted features and mold-ed hair. The 12" doll on right looks like a Petite Sally copy, $125-$150. The smaller doll is 10", $100-$125.

Googly-Eyed-Type Doll with cloth body and legs, composition head with painted features, 9", $225-$300. Courtesy of Lynnae Ramsey.

Right: Unmarked composition Girl with beautiful blue sleep eyes, cloth body; composition head, arms and legs; opened mouth, 20", $175-$200. Author's Collection.

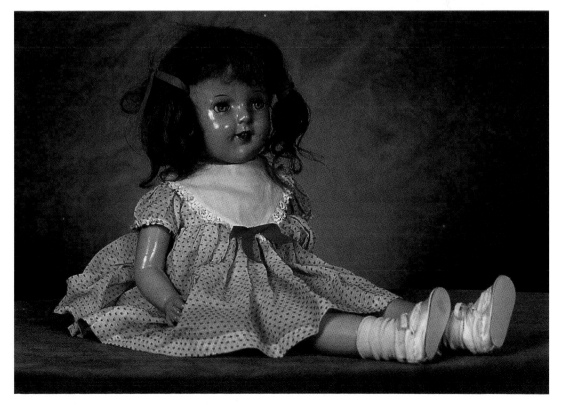

Above Left: Russian Composition Child; composition head, blue sleep eyes with real lashes, closed mouth, mohair wig, 26", $300-$500. Courtesy of McMaster's Doll Auction.

Above Right: Composition Red Riding Hood, 11", painted features, original clothing, with Heidi, 8", composition with painted features; both dolls have a five-piece composition body and mohair wig, $75-$100 each. Courtesy of McMaster's Doll Auction.

Left: Composition Girl with blue tin sleep eyes, human hair wig, five-piece composition body, dressed in original blue outfit, 14", $100-$200. Courtesy of McMaster's Doll Auction.

Right: Attributed to Raleigh, an all composition Boy with fine finished accents around toes and face, redressed, $600 and up. Courtesy of Pat Wood.

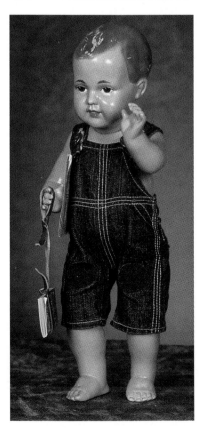

German wooden Soldiers with Castle, made in late 1800s. Soldiers and Horses have hand-painted features; Castle has lithographed design on outside; $300 and up. Courtesy of James & Judy Sneed.

Soldiers and Sailors with Cannon. All wood-jointed with painted features and metal guns, they look similar to Jaymar Toys, but are unmarked; $75-$100. Courtesy of Ronnie Kauk.

Above Left: Unmarked Mannequin Doll, jointed at shoulders only, molded head, painted features, 13", $50-$100. Courtesy of Lisa Sheets.

Bottom Left: Mannequin Doll, all composition, jointed at arms and legs, 36", molded hair, painted features with painted mouth, $300 and up. Courtesy of Seaview Antique Dolls.

Above: Unmarked Duck Pull Toy—possibly made by Hustler Toy Company, $50-$75. Courtesy of James & Judy Sneed.

Bottom: Wooden Dog Pull Toy, painted eyes and mouth, painted body and collar, notches on collar, metal pieces to hold on legs, wooden wheels and ears, $50-$75. Courtesy of James & Judy Sneed.

Great Pull Toy of Little Boy on Bike, wood-beaded legs and arms, painted smiling face, baseball hat; legs go up and down when pulled by string; $50-$75. Courtesy of James & Judy Sneed.

All wood Rocking Horse on orange and green base; horse nicely painted with carousel-type markings; $35-$75. Courtesy of James & Judy Sneed.

Wood Pull Toy with Lady sitting on metal bars on wooden base, painted features; woman moves back and forth when pulled; $50-$75. Courtesy of James & Judy Sneed.

Darling Cat Pull Toy, 1930s, all wood except for bell and screws, red and green with black cats, white painted features; cats go up and down and bell rings when pulled; $50-$100. Courtesy of James & Judy Sneed.

Above: Bed Doll with composition head and hands; cloth body, arms, and legs; dramatic painted features, $80-$125.

Right: Unmarked Oriental-Style Boy Doll with composition and molded head, cloth body and limbs, original clothing, painted features, $200-$300. Courtesy of Annette's Antique Dolls.

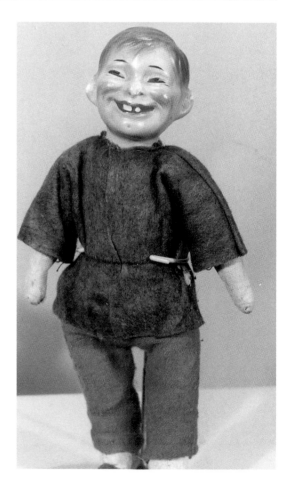

Unusual Uncle Sam Doll; composition head, cloth body and limbs, painted features; in this condition, $250; in mint condition, $500 and up.

Noah's Ark, late 1800s; top opens up to hold animals; 27" long, all wood with painted features, excellent piece with many animals in very good condition, $750 and up. Courtesy of James & Judy Sneed.

Dream Babies, composition with opened mouth, 11"; one seated with sleep eyes; one standing with painted eyes. Courtesy of Lynnae Ramsey.

CHAPTER FOURTEEN
SOME OF THE REST

❦

AMERICAN CHARACTER DOLL CO.
New York, New York, U.S.A., 1919-On
Marked "Petite" or "Petite Doll"

PETITE SALLY
Far Left: Marked "Petite Sally," has composition head, arms, and legs with cloth body, $225-$275. Courtesy of Susan Killoran.

Bottom: Close-up of marking on head of Petite Sally.

Left: Tin-eyed Sally. This doll was made to compete with the Patsy line of dolls, $250-$350. Courtesy of Pat Wood.

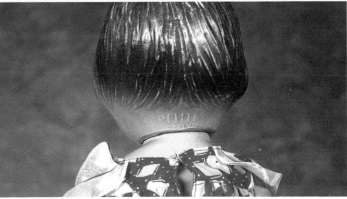

PUGGY—1928

Composition with molded and painted hair, pug nose, closed mouth, eyes look to side; marked "A PETITE DOLL," 12", $400-$500 (See Chapter 4, "Black Composition Dolls," for photo of Black Puggy).

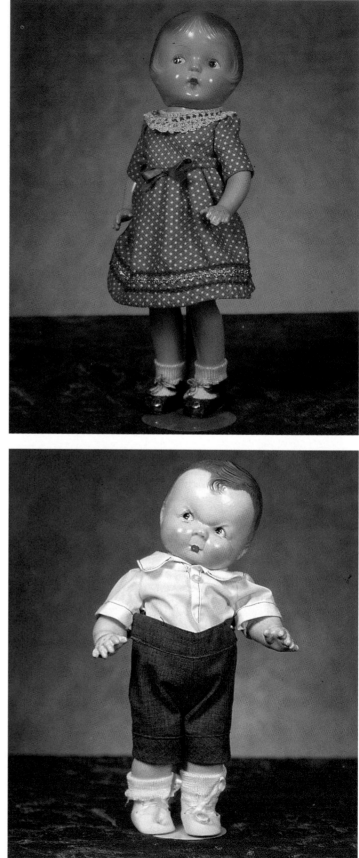

Above Right: Petite Nancy, painted features, molded hair, 12", $225-$250.

Above Top: Tin-eyed Sally. Unmarked 18" composition Girl with sleep eyes and painted mouth, believed to be American Character. Courtesy of Pat Wood.

Above Bottom: Campbell's Kids ad for a Petite Doll of the Campbell's Kid. Courtesy of Judd Larson.

Above: Puggy. Courtesy of Lynnae Ramsey (See Chapter 4, "Black Composition Dolls").

ARRANBEE OR R & B

U.S.A., 1922-1960

Marked "R & B" or "ARRANBEE"

Left: Nancy, composition, sleep eyes, 19", $275. Author's Collection.

Right: Nancy, 13", marked with an X with a circle around it; all composition with sleep eyes, mohair wig, all original yellow outfit, $250. Courtesy of Pat Wood.

DEBU'TEEN DOLLS were marked "Debu'Teen, R & B Quality Doll" on paper tag, "Debu'Teen" on paper label on end of boxes. They have recently grown in popularity, and the prices have reflected that increased interest.

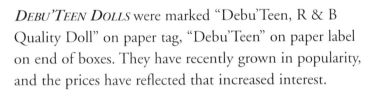

Left: Debu'Teen, all original with box, $375 and up. Courtesy of Pat Wood.

Right: Debu'Teen, all original, $300 and up. Courtesy of Sharron's Dolls.

Far Left: R & B WAC Doll in original outfit, composition head with five-piece composition body, human hair wig, blue sleep eyes (WAC stands for Woman's Army Corp.); she is marked "R & B" on back of head; 17", $300-$400. Courtesy of McMaster's Doll Auction.

Left: Debu'Teen in original Cowgirl outfit with box, she has blue tin sleep eyes, composition head, red mohair wig, five-piece composition body, closed mouth, $450 and up. Courtesy of McMaster's Doll Auction.

Bottom Left: R & B Princess Elizabeth, all original with box; box is marked "Nanette," but it was marked out, and "Princess Elizabeth" written in. Many times in department stores, boxes would get switched, and they would sell one doll in another box. R & B also produced Nannette (her head and body were marked "Nancy") another popular R & B doll. $350 and up. Courtesy of Pat Wood.

Bottom: Debu'Teen in original ski outfit with skis, gray and white outfit with matching hat, leather straps on skies, $300 and up.

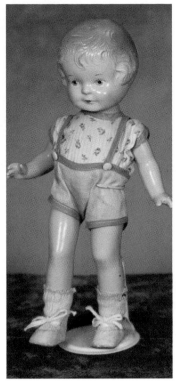

Above Left: Arranbee Nancy, all original and excellent, sleep eyes, 20", $350-$400. Courtesy of Pat Wood.

Above: Composition Boy, 12", $150-$175. Courtesy of Pat Wood.

Above Right: Nancy, 18", all original. Courtesy of Pat Wood.

Left: Debu'Teen, all original in skating outfit, 12", $300 and up. Courtesy of Pat Wood.

Right: Sonja Henie, made by the R & B Company; 20", $400-$450. Courtesy of Lynnae Ramsey.

BYE-LO BABY BY GRACE PUTNAM

Composition head with cloth body and celluloid hands. The composition heads were made by Cameo Doll Co.; wooden heads by the Schoenhut Company; the bodies supplied by K & K Toy Co., and Konig & Wernicke. Made from 1922 on, these dolls are measured by their head circumference. Geo. Borgfeldt & Co. was the sole distributor for the K & K Bye-Lo Babies. They came in sizes from 9" to 20".

10", $425-$500. Courtesy of Sunnie Newell.

Five-piece composition body, all original. (This Grace Putnam Bye-Lo Baby went at auction for $2,000.) Courtesy of Pat Wood.

Left: 12", with original outfit, $250-$600. Some rare outfits can command prices up to $1,000. Author's Collection.

Right: Buddy Lee Ride 'Em Cowboy! $500 and up. Courtesy of Pat Wood.

Buddy Lee in rare New York Central Lines outfit, all original, $1,000 and up.

Buddy Lee with original denim outfit with cap, painted features, all composition with painted boots.

Buddy Lee; cap and pants labeled "Union Made, Lee, Sanforized, Shrunk;" Lee-snaps on front of pants; all composition with molded and painted boots, painted features; $400. Courtesy of McMaster's Doll Auction.

CENTURY DOLL COMPANY
New York, New York, 1909-On
Made Bisque and Composition Dolls.

CHUCKLES (NOT PICTURED)
Composition head, shoulder plates, composition arms and legs, cloth bodies, tin eyes; 18", $250-$275; 23", $350-$375.

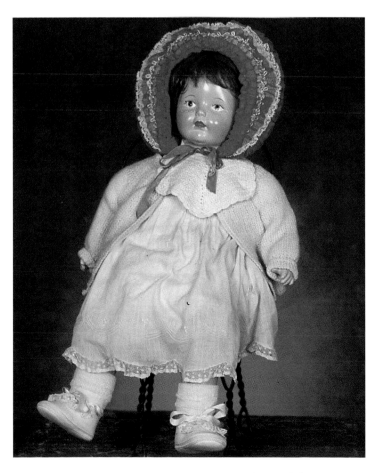

Right: Century Mama Doll, composition with closed mouth, cloth body with crier, painted eyes, 21", $275-$350. Courtesy of Pat Wood.

FREUNDLICH NOVELTY CORP.—1923-0n

Above: General Douglas MacArthur Doll, all original, came with paper tag that read, "General MacAthur, Made in 1942;" all composition with molded hat, painted features, 18", $275-$325. Author's Collection.

Right Top & Middle: Little Red Riding Hood with Grandmother and the Wolf. Shown with lithographed School House box, dolls are composition with molded heads and painted features, all originally dressed; circa 1940; $375 and up. Courtesy of Robert DeCenzo.

Right Bottom: The Big Bad Wolf and the Three Pigs, circa 1935; all have molded heads and five-piece composition bodies, painted features; shown with original box; $475 and up. Courtesy of Rosalie Whyle Museum of Doll Art.

BABY SANDY

Made from 1939-1942. Composition, jointed at shoulders and hips, molded hair, swivel head; marked on head, "Baby Sandy."

8" with painted eyes, $150-$175.
12" with sleep eyes, $200-$230.
14"-15" with sleep eyes, $300-$350.
17" with sleep eyes, $350-$375.

Inset Photo: Baby Sandy, 17". Courtesy of Lynnae Ramsey.

15" Baby Sandy. Courtesy of Sunnie Newell.

GEORGENE AVERILL (MADAME HENDREN)
New York, New York
Dolly Reckord 1922; record player in body; composition head, arms, and legs with cloth body; 26", $500-$600.

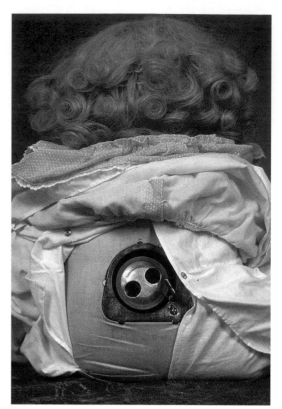

Left: Dolly Reckord. Courtesy of Lynnae Ramsey.

Right: Record Playing mechanism in the Dolly Reckord Doll; identical to the Mae Starr Doll.

HAZELLE'S MARIONETTES
They were marketed as realistic, educational, entertaining, and nonbreakable.

The Big Bad Wolf and Grandmother, made with composition head, feet, and hands; cloth bodies, painted features; with their original boxes; sticks to move the limbs were marked "HAZELLE'S MARIONETTES, K.D. MO PATENT (with number), Made in USA," $50-$125 each. Courtesy of Annette's Antique Dolls.

Hazelle's Marionettes—Black Girl, Bunny, and Clown—all with composition heads, feet, and hands; cloth bodies; Clown and Bunny have molded heads; Black Girl has mohair wig; all with original boxes, $50-$125; shown with Minnie Mouse Marionette (unmarked, but looks like a Pellum Puppet) $125. Courtesy of Annette's Antique Dolls.

Horsman—E.I. Horsman Co.

New York, New York, Late 1800s-On
Founded by Edward Imeson Horsman
Marked "E.I.H.//CO."

BILLIKEN

Made in 1909. Composition head, slits for eyes, velvet or plush body, marked "Billiken" on foot, 12", $325-$400.

Billiken. Courtesy of Sunnie Newell.

Horsman's Groom Doll, dressed in black tuxedo with white shirt and bow, sleep eyes, painted lashes, opened mouth, mohair wig; shown with 20" Deanna Durbin Bride Doll, 20", $300-$400. Courtesy of McMaster's Doll Auction.

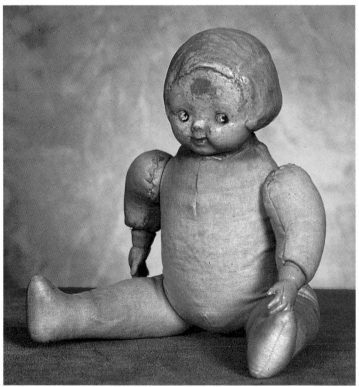

Campbell's Kid, marked "c1910," composition with straw-filled arms and body, molded hair, painted features, 11", $150-$175. Author's Collection.

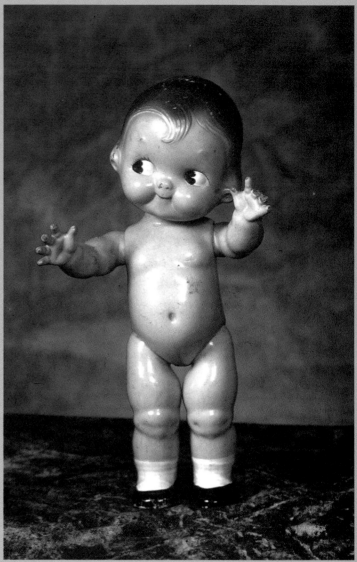

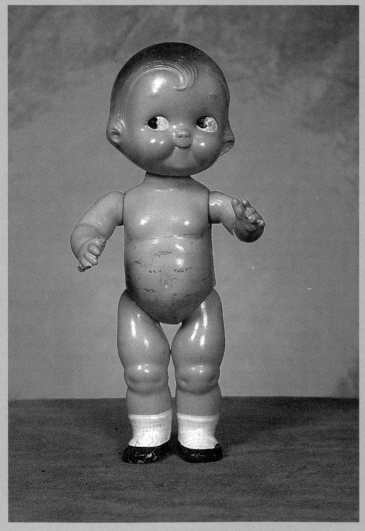

Top Left: Two cute Campbell's Kids. Courtesy of Carl Kludt.

Above: Campbell's Kid, all composition with painted features (cute as can be), $350. Author's Collection.

Left: Campbell's Kid, all composition, painted features; molded, painted hair; watermelon mouth; 12", $300-$350.

Ads for Campbell's Soup using the Campbell Kids. Courtesy of Nineteenth Century Imprints, Elisabeth Burdon.

Left: All original Campbell's Kid in cooking outfit with original paper tag which reads, "Campbell's Kid," A HORSMAN DOLL, Permission of Campbell's Soup Company," $350-$400. Courtesy of Marci.

DIMPLES

Composition head, molded & painted hair; opened mouth, smiling; tin eyes, cloth body with composition arms and legs; 16"-18", $250-$300; 22"-24", $350-$425.

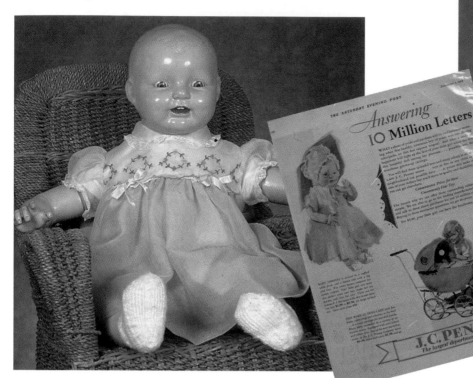

Dimples, 24". Courtesy of Lynnae Ramsey.

Center: Ad for Horsman's Baby Dimples being sold at J.C. Penney.

HeBee, SheBee, 1925. This one is a SheBee. Their shoes were painted blue or pink, and came with a matching ribbon laced in the shoes. All composition, closed mouth with painted eyes, 11" tall; $250-$335, in fair condition; $550 and up, in excellent condition. Author's Collection.

HOUSE OF PUZZY

The House of Puzzy designed and sold only two dolls: 14" Sizzy ($300-$400) and 15" Puzzy ($375-$450). They were a brother and sister team manufactured in 1948 by Herman Colin in Baltimore, Maryland. All composition with painted features and molded heads; marked "Puzzy c, H of P. USA."

Left: Puzzy is the boy on right; Sizzy is the girl on left. Courtesy of Sunnie Newell.

Right: Side view showing the molding of the heads.

MARY HOYER DOLL MANUFACTURING COMPANY

Reading, Pennsylvania, 1925-On
Designed by Bernard Lipfert
Marked "The Mary Hoyer Doll" or "ORIGINAL Mary
Hoyer Doll"

*Marked on torso "The Mary Hoyer Doll," or in a circle marked
"ORIGINAL Mary Hoyer Doll." These dolls were originally made
in composition, then later changed to hard plastic.*

Composition, 14", $325-$400.
Hard Plastic, 14", $350-$425.
Boy, with wig, 14, $450-$525.
Gigi, 18", $550-$650.

*Above: Close-up of a beautiful Mary Hoyer Doll, all original with
box.*

*Above Left: Mary Hoyer, all original, 14". Courtesy of Lynnae
Ramsey.*

*Above Right: All original Mary Hoyer with original box. Courtesy
of Pat Wood.*

*Above Right: Mary Hoyer Doll, all original with box. Courtesy of
Sharron's Dolls.*

MISCELLANEOUS

LOUIS AMBERG & SONS, 1878-1930
Cincinnati, Ohio; New York, New York

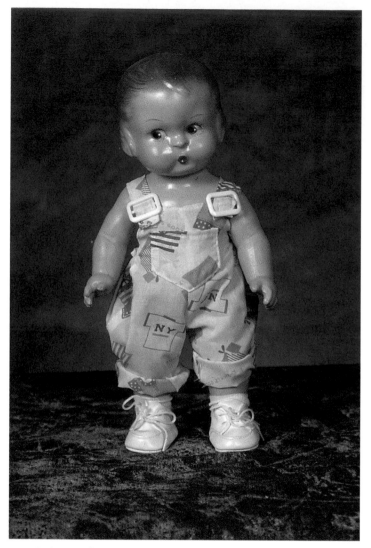

Marked "L.A.&S. C 1928," Sue, Edwina or It: All composition with molded and painted hair, painted eyes, all original, 14", $375-$425; redressed, $275. Courtesy of Sunnie Newell.

EEGEE DOLL COMPANY
Brooklyn, New York, 1917-On

Marked "EEGEE" or "TRADEMARK EEGEE DOLLS MADE IN USA"

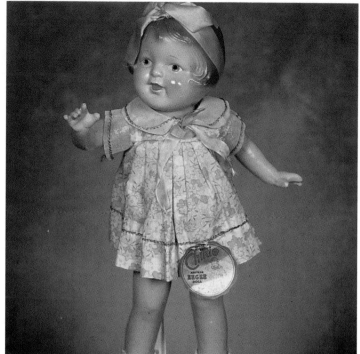

Chikie by Eegee, with tag, museum quality; all original; 16", $395.

EUGENAIL DOLL COMPANY

Composition Girl, all original, with sleep eyes and cute smile; 16", $250-$350. Courtesy of Pat Wood.

INTERNATIONAL DOLL

Composition World's Fair Doll, 20", 1939, with original World's Fair dress and scarf, brown sleep eyes, five-piece composition body; paper wrist tag reads, "New York World's Fair 1939 Inc., Officially Licensed, © NYWF." Dressed marked "International Doll, Reg. U.S. Pat Off, Officially Licensed, New York World's Fair, A Joy Doll Product." Included is her original orange box. Sold at McMaster's Doll Auction in 1997 for $410. Courtesy of McMaster's Doll Auctions.

K & W, PS

Composition Toddler from Russia, 20"; marked "PS (intertwined), 2966, 11, 0" on back of head, "55 lightly molded" on left shoulder. Painted bisque composition head, blue sleep eyes, opened mouth, synthetic wig, five-piece composition toddler body with crier, original outfit. Shown with 23" composition Russian Girl marked "K & W, 155/10" on head, "K & W, 52" on back; flirty, blue sleep eyes with tin lids; real lashes, opened mouth, synthetic curly wig, five-piece composition body with crier; dressed in original outfit, $100-$200 each. Courtesy of McMaster's Doll Auctions.

QUAN QUAN COMPANY OF LOS ANGELES

Ming Ming Baby, all composition, oriental costume, painted feet, 9", $175-$200. Collection of Sunnie Newell.

Marked "20 *" This pretty composition Girl is 19" tall, $175. Susan Killoran Collection.

Marked "Germany 378 4 1/2" on head, all composition with painted eyes, 21", $250-$350. Author's Collection.

PLAYSKOOL

TERRI LEE SALES CORP.

Playskool wooden toy, showing four happy fellows with wooden heads and bodies; hit the colored stick in front of the people, and they will pop up and hit the bell; $25-$50.

Composition, with painted features, redressed, 14", $350-$400. Author's Collection.

MONICA DOLL STUDIOS
Hollywood, CA.

The Monica Dolls were made with human, rooted hair. They were manufactured from 1941-1951. All composition with a swivel head, painted eyes, closed mouth. They were unmarked and came in several sizes: 11", 15", 17", 20", 22", and 24"; box was marked "Monica of Hollywood." First announced in *Toys and Novelty* magazine in 1941, she was designed by Mrs. Hansi Share—who developed her so there would be a doll with hair that children could brush. $350-$475.

Above: Redressed Monica, 20". Courtesy of Sunnie Newell.

Top Right: Two sizes of Monica Dolls with different hair color. Courtesy of Lennae Ramsey.

Bottom Right: Monica in original wedding dress with veil. Author's Collection.

PELHAM PUPPETS
ENGLAND

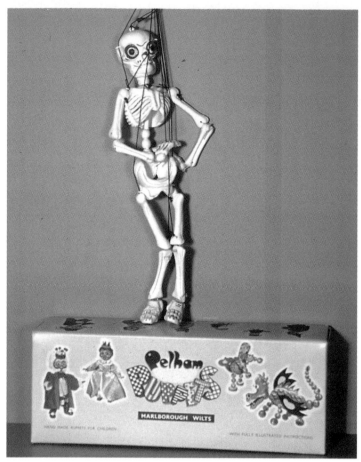

Donald and Snoopy's little sidekick, Woodstock. Donald, $125-$150; Woodstock, $75-$125. Courtesy of Gasoline Alley.

Above: Another unusual Pelham Puppet, $75-$125. This Skeleton is sure to scare you! Courtesy of Gasoline Alley.

Below: Pirate and Witch, $75-$125. Courtesy of Gasoline Alley.

Unusual Dragon, dramatic colors, $100. Courtesy of Gasoline Alley.

A rare Pelham Puppet Disney Store Display. This animated piece features Goofy, Mickey, Donald, Minnie, and Pluto. On a wooden base, the characters have painted features with coordinating clothing. The mechanism to pull the strings is located on the top of the display under the fringed pieces. It is marked "Walt Disney Productions." A very nice piece; $2,500-$3,500. Author's Collection.

Right: Pinocchio Pelham Puppet store display piece, standing over two feet tall, $750 and up.

W.S. REED CO.
Leominster, Massachusetts

W.S. Reed Company manufactured a large variety of wooden toys for children from 1875 to around 1910. The company was also a chair manufacturer. One of its most popular toys was the Gigantic Circus and Mammoth Hippodrome which showed many circus acrobats and animals painted with bright colors.

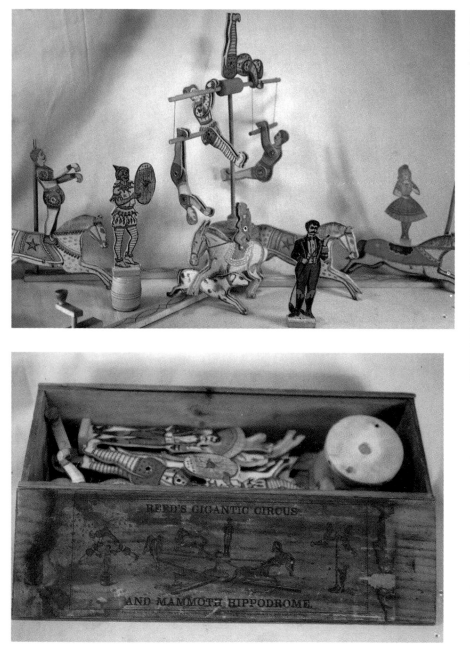

Top Right: This shows the large fold-out sheet that was enclosed in the box for the Hippodrome. A complete set can sell for over $2,000. Courtesy of Robert DeCenzo.

Top Left: Made in 1885, this is a good shot of the wonderful Circus Characters that are part of the Gigantic Circus and Mammoth Hippodrome collection. Courtesy of Robert DeCenzo.

Bottom Left: The original box which held the Circus pieces. Courtesy of Robert DeCenzo.

Here are close-up versions of the Circus pieces that were part of Reed's Gigantic Circus and Mammoth Hippodrome. All photos courtesy of James & Judy Sneed.

Little Wonder Trolley Car, Circa 1895, wood and lithographed toy train with bright colors, nice piece, $350 and up. Courtesy of Robert DeCenzo.

ABC Letter Blocks, circa 1895, wood with lithograph in original box, $300 and up. Courtesy of Robert DeCenzo.

Jack-in-the-Box, Teddy Roosevelt, circa 1900, composition head and molded hat with wooden box, $500 and up. Courtesy of Robert DeCenzo.

RELIABLE TOY COMPANY
Toronto, Canada, 1920-On
Marked "RELIABLE MADE IN CANADA"
Hiawatha, 13", $75-$125.
Scottish Girl, 14", $75-$100.
Military Man, 14", $175-$250.
Aviator, 14", $225-$275.
Mountie, 17", $300-$325.

Above Right: Scottish Boy, all composition with painted features, 13", $125-$150. Courtesy of Sunnie Newell.

Right: Composition, all original, marked "Reliable Doll Co. Canada 450 Her Highness Coronation Co." This doll was made from the Barbara Ann Scott Doll. Barbara Ann Scott was a Canadian Skater. It was made in honor of the Queen's Coronation; 15", $450 and up. Courtesy of Pat Wood.

Middle Right: Composition with molded hair and tin sleep eyes, 18", $75. Courtesy of Susan Killoran.

Bottom Right: Gentleman, same face as Aviator, composition head, cloth body, painted features, $125-$150. Courtesy of Sunnie Newell.

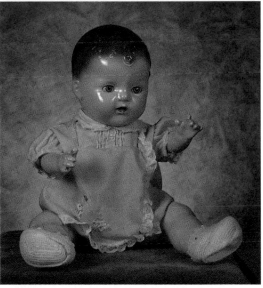

TALENTOY BY TALENT PRODUCTS INC.

New York, New York
Puppets, $75-$125 each.

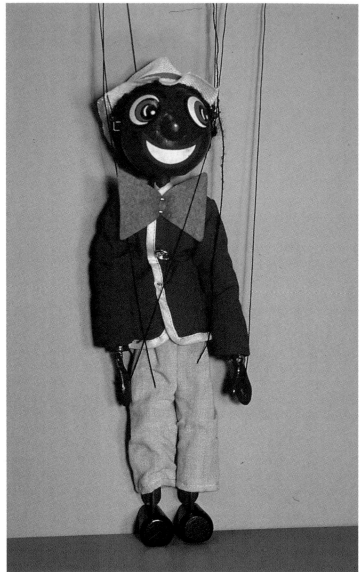

Top Left: Close-up of record that came with puppets. Courtesy of Gasoline Alley.

Middle Left: Clown Puppet named Pim-Bo the Clown. Courtesy of Gasoline Alley.

Bottom Left: Record with Cover. Courtesy of Gasoline Alley.

Above: Jambo the Jiver. Courtesy of Gasoline Alley.

Talentoy Record showing a close-up of all the puppets used in this series. Courtesy of Gasoline Alley.

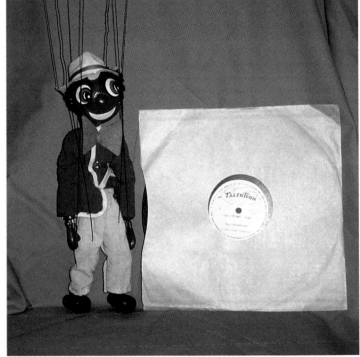

Black Puppet named Jambo the Jiver, with record. Courtesy of Gasoline Alley.

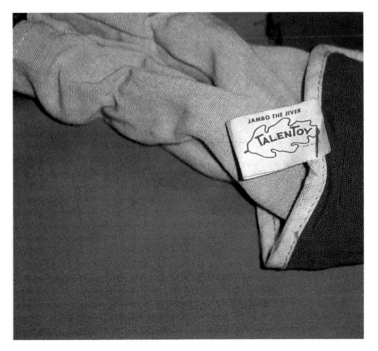

Talentoy Label attached to puppets. Courtesy of Gasoline Alley.

Black Puppet named Toonga from the Congo, with record. Puppet, $75-$125. Courtesy of Gasoline Alley.

TWISTUM TOY FACTORY
Oakland, California

Cat with molded composition head, wooden body, and painted features; 3 1/4" long; marked "Patent Applied For Twistum Toy Factory Oakland, CA." $25-$75. Courtesy of Ronnie Kauk.

Bulldog with molded composition head and legs, center body is wood, painted features, marked "Patent Applied For Twistum Toy Factory Oakland, CA." $25-$50. Courtesy of Ronnie Kauk.

VOGUE DOLLS, INC.
Medford, Massachusetts

Created by Jennie Graves; clothes by Virginia Graves; clothes tagged "Vogue Dolls" or
"VOGUE DOLLS, INC. MEDFORD, MASS.USA REG U.S. PAT OFF" or "Vogue."

Vogue Toddles Gretel, 7 1/2", painted features, five-piece composition body, composition head, mohair wig, $125-$175, shown with Vogue Toddles Aviator in original outfit with painted features, five-piece composition body, composition head, $350-$400. Courtesy of McMaster's Doll Auction.

> **DOLLS NOT PICTURED**
>
> **LITTLE ORPHAN ANNIE**
> 12", $275-$350.
> *(See Chapter 2, "Character Dolls & Toys")*
>
> **CHARLIE CHAPLIN**
> *(See Chapter 2, "Character Dolls & Toys")*

Vogue Toddles, all original with box, painted features, 8", $250-$300. Courtesy of Pat Wood.

Vogue Betty Jane, 1940's unmarked doll with sleep eyes; 13", $300-$375. Courtesy of Pat Wood.

INDEX

African Chief 162

Alexander (Dagwood's Son) 27

Alexander (Madame) 56, 126-155

Alice in Wonderland 28, 139

Alligator 164

Alt, Beck & Gottschalack 13

Amberg, Louis & Sons 214

American Character 57, 199

American Children 62, 67

American Merchandise Distributors 39

Amish Couple 62

Amos 104

Andy 104, 105

Anne Shirley .62, 63, 67

Arabian Camel 164

Arranbee or R & B 141, 201-203

Aviator 223, 226

Baby 23, 72, 182, 186

Baby Adele 23

Baby Blossom 13

Baby Bo-Kaye 10, 13

Baby Bundie 10, 13, 22

Baby Dimples 212

Baby Grumpy 64

Baby McGuffy 140

Baby Mine 23

Baby Sandy 207

Baby Snooks (Fanny Brice) 13, 22, 85

Baby Tinyette 72

Baby Weens 19

Bambi 42

Bandy (Bandmaster) 13, 14

Barbara Ann 62, 74

Barbara Ann Scott (Her Royal Highness) 223

Barbara Joan 62, 74

Barbara Lou 62, 74

Barney & Spark Plug 160

Barney Google 38, 160, 161

Baseball Player 12

Bear 110, 165

Bed Doll 196

Betsy Wetsy 90

Bette 18

Betty Boop 11, 13, 14, 28

Betty Brite 74

Betty Jane 90

Betty Roll Duck 78, 79

Big Bad Wolf 206, 208

Billiken 209

Billy 80

Bimbo 11, 13, 14

Birnblick Toy Co. 18

Black Dolls 52-59, 63, 74, 75

Bo-Fair 13, 22

Bones (Ginger, Bones, & Streak) 13

Bonzo 13, 22, 28

Boob McNutt 161

Boy Blue 138

Boy Doll 181, 182, 187, 190

Bride Doll 138

Bridesmaid 141

Bright Eyes 64, 98

Bronco Bill 118

Brother Baby Coos 90

Bubbles 13, 65

Buddy Lee 204, 205

Bulldog 226

Butch 140

Buster Brown 30

Bye-Lo Baby 23, 204

Camel 80, 164

Cameo Doll Co. 8-25

Campbell's Kids 200, 209-211

Captain January 98

Carmen 138

Cat 13, 15, 194, 226

Century Doll Company 205

Champ 13, 22

Character Dolls & Toys 26-39

Charlie Chaplin 29, 214

Charlie McCarthy 29, 66, 105

Chein 35

Chikie 214

Chinaman 108, 112

Chuckles 205

Circus Riders 168, 169

Circus Tent 171

Clothes Pin Doll 185

Clown 85, 166, 167

Comical Mouse 112

Crown Toy Co. 49

Crownie 13, 15

Cynthia 56, 154

Curly Top 98

Curly Kayoe 29

Davy Crockett 29, 120

Debu'Teen 201-203

Dolly Reckord 208

Deanna Durbin 82, 83, 90, 209

Denny Dimwit 30

Dewees Cochran 62

Dick Tracy 30

Dionne Quintuplets 127-137

Dimples 212

Disney 15, 40-51, 84, 86, 89, 119-121, 125, 154, 219

Doctor Dafoe 127, 132

Dog 13, 15, 30, 105, 194

Dollie 13, 22

Donald Duck 40, 42, 43, 106, 121, 218, 219

Donkey 118

Dopey 44, 219

Dragon 218

Dream Baby 198

Duck 81, 194

Dy-Dee Baby 130

Dye-A-Babe 23

Dumbo 13, 15, 19, 44

Ed Wynn 108

Edgar Bergen 66

Eegee Doll Company 214

Elephant 110, 121, 168, 169, 185

Effanbee 16, 57, 60-75

Eugenail Doll Company 214

Fanny Brice (Baby Snooks) 13, 22, 85

FAO Schwarz 61, 71

Felix the Cat 13, 15, 23, 31, 157

Ferdinand the Bull 30, 84

Figaro 45

Fisher Price 51

Fleischaker & Baum 130

Flexy's 85

Flexy Soldier 85

Flora McFlimsey 141

Flossie Flirt 90

Flub-A-Dub 124, 125

Foxy 32

Foxy Grandpa Roly-Poly 181

Frantz Mfg. 77

Fran-zell the Dog 80

Freundlich Novelty Corp. 33, 206

Fun-E-Flex 43, 46, 47, 51

Funny Frog 112

Gabby 84

Galloping Jockey 176, 179

Gator 110

Geo. Borgfeldt Corp. 9, 10, 13, 22, 23, 47, 51, 54

General Douglas MacArthur 206

General Electric 14

Gentleman 223

Geogene Averill (Madame Hendren) 208

Giant Galloping Jockey 179

Giggles 13, 15

Ginger 13

Ginger, Bones, Streak 13

Giraffe 111, 165

Girl Dolls 182, 184-187, 190-192, 216

Gloria Ann 74

Goat 162, 167

Googly-Eyed Dolls 55, 56, 190, 191

Grace Drayton 37

Groom Doll 209

Grace Putnam 23, 204

Hazelle's Marionettes 208

Hawaiian Shirley 97

Heart Beat Baby 74

HeBee, SheBee 212

Herby 32

Hiawatha 223

Hippodrome 221, 222

Hiram 78

Historical Series 67

Hit & Miss 120

Hobo 169

Honey 74

Ho-Ho 23

Horse 171, 194

Horsman E.I. Horsman Co. 209-212

Hotpoint Man (Happy Hotpoint) 13, 16

House of Puzzy 212

Howdy Doody 13, 16, 32, 84, 117

Humphrey Mobile 86

Humpty Dumpty 112

Humpty Dumpty Circus 170

Hustler Bell Hop 76, 77

Hustler Toy Co. 76-81

Hustler Twins 77

Hustler Watch Dog 81

Ideal Toy Corporation 18, 21, 22, 45, 82-99, 130

Ignatz 106

Indian 109, 112

Indian Chief 119

International Doll Company 215

Jack-in-the-Box Teddy Roosevelt 222

Jack Collins 17

Jackie Robinson 54

Jambo the Jiver 224, 225

Jane Withers 142

Jaymar 100-115

JC Penney 61, 71

Jeannie Walker 143

Jeep 13, 17, 102

Jennie Graves 226

Jerry Mahoney 26, 27

Jester 108

Jiggs 32, 106, 160, 161

Jiminy Cricket 13, 22, 45, 86

Princess Elizabeth

Jimmy Durante's Friend (Umbriago) 39

Joe Palooka 86, 104

Joseph Kallus 9-12, 18, 19, 22-24, 44, 84, 89

Joy 11, 13, 17

Judy Garland 83, 87, 90

K & K Toy Company 13

Kayo 107, 112

Kewpie 9, 24

Kewpidoodle Dog 24

King Features Syndicate 17, 21, 102

Kohner 116-125

Konig & Wericke 23

Knickerbocker 27, 45, 50

Komical Kop 112

Krazy Kat 32, 106

Lady 188

Lady Acrobat 168

Lanky Tinker 174

Leopard 164, 168

Liberty Boy 88

Lion 171

Little Annie Rooney 13, 17

Little Betty 140

Little Colonel 96, 99

Little Girl 68

Little King 13, 18, 90, 115

Little Lady 63, 68

Little Nemo's Dr. Pimm 161

Little Orphan Annie 33, 86, 101, 112, 206

Little Pig 105

Lone Ranger 37, 118

Loony Links 122

Louis Amberg & Sons 214

Lovums 68

Lucky Lindy 34

Lucky The Cat 123

Mac The Sailor 121

Mad Hatter 34

Madeleine 144

Mae Starr 69

Maggie (Jiggs) 160, 161

Magic Skin Baby 90

Make Your Own Funnies 112

Mama Dolls 60, 90, 205

Mama Katzenjammer 38

Mammy Dolls 54

Man 114

Mannequin 194

Marcella 144

Marcia 11, 13, 18

Margaret O'Brien 143, 144

Margie 13, 18, 23

Marilee 74

Mary Hoyer 213

Mary Lee 70

Mammy (Tony Sarg) 155

Marilyn Knowlden 99

Mary Pickford 17

May & Moritz 34

McGuffy Ana 145

Mickey 70

Mickey Mouse 13, 19, 41, 42, 46, 47, 125, 219

Micky 47

Military Man 223

Ming Ming 216

Minnie Mouse 46, 47, 113, 208, 219

Miss America 90, 146

Miss Curity 38, 88

Miss Liberty 87, 90

Miss USO 90

Miss Peep 23

Molly E 52, 53

Monica Doll Studios 217

Moon Mullins 107, 112

Mordimer Snerd 85

Mountie 223

Mr. Peanut 13, 20

Mutual Doll Company 10

Nancy 141, 201, 203

Negro Dude 163

Noah's Ark 197

Noma Electric 16, 61

Now & Forever 98

Nurse Doll 132, 188

Occident Flour Man 100

Olive Oyl 102

Oriental-Style Doll 196

Ostrich 111, 165

Our Little Girl 98

Paco 48

Panchito 48

Pat Sullivan 157

Patricia 70

Patricia Kin 70, 74, 75

Patsy Baby 72

Patsyette 70, 72

Patsy 70, 71

Patsy Ann 70, 72

Patsy Babyette 70, 73

Patsy Joan 61, 70, 73

Patsy Jr. 70, 72

Patsy Lou 70, 73, 74

Patsy Mae 70, 74

Patsy Ruth 70, 74

Patsy Tinyette 70, 72

Patsy Type 57, 59, 180, 185

Peanut 23

Pelham Puppets 208, 218, 219

Penguin 51

Pete the Pup 8, 11, 13, 20

Peter Pan 34, 119

Peter Puppet Playthings 28

Petite Doll 200

Petite Nancy 200

Petite Sally 199, 200

Pim-Bo the Clown 224

Pinkie 13, 21, 23

Pinocchio 13, 21, 45, 49, 89, 111, 219

Pirate 218

Playskool 216

Plassie 90

Pluto 42, 51, 219

Policeman 35, 109

Poncho Hustler 81

Poor Little Rich Girl 98

Popeye 13, 21, 23, 35, 102, 103, 112

Popeye's Dog (Jeep) 17

Prince Charming 146

Princess Elizabeth 130, 146, 147, 202

Princess Summerfall Winterspring 121

Puggy 57, 200

Punch & Judy 36

Puppy Pippin 37

Puss'n'Boots 104

Puzzy 212

Quan Quan Company 216

R & B or Arranbee 141, 201-203

Raleigh 192

Ranger Shirley 99

RCA Radiotron 13, 22

Red Goose 112

Red Riding Hood 192, 206

Reed (W.S.) Reed Company 221, 222

Reliable Toy Company 223

Rex Company 9

Ring-A-Ling 113

Ringmaster 162

Rocking Horse 195

Rooster 109

Rose O'Neill 9, 10, 15, 25

Rosemary 57, 74

Rudolph the Reindeer 125

Russian Dolls 192, 215

Sad Sack 39

Sailor 12, 14, 193

Sally-Sallykins 90

Sam 85

Sambo 78

Sandy 86, 110, 112

Santa 13, 22

Santa Clause 120

Scrappy 39

Scarlett O'Hara . . . . 148, 149, cover

Schoenhut Dolls & Toys 15, 156-171

Scootles 23, 25

Scott Girl 223

Scottish Girl 154

Scottish Boy 223

Seven Dwarfs 45, 50, 89

Shirley Temple 90-97, 99, 130, 151, 159

Shirley Temple-type 58, 183, 186-188

Sissie 13, 22

Sizzie 212

Skeleton 218

Skier 105

Skippy 70, 75

Snoozie 90

Snowman 113

Snow White 50, 89, 149

Soldier 108, 156, 198

Sonja Henie 126, 139, 150-153, 203

Spanish Girl 154

Spark Plug 38

Special Girl 154

Spinning Jack Tinker 174

Streak (Ginger, Bones, & Streak) 16

Sue, Edwina, or It 214

Sunny Sue 85

Superman 13, 22, 38, 89

Suzanne 74

Suzette 74

Sweetie Pie 74

Syrocco 38

Talentoy 224, 225

Ted Toy Express 175

Ted Toyler Inc 172-179

Teddy Roosevelt Jack-in-the-Box 222

Teddy Soldier 172, 173, 175-177

Terry Lee Sales Corp. 216

The Drunk 123

The Three Pigs 51, 206

Tickletoes 90

Timothy Mouse 13, 19

Tinker Dogs 178

Tinker Mule 179

Tinker Toy 174, 178

Tipsy Tom 120

Toby 37

Tommy Tucker 74

Tonto 37

Tony Sarg Marionettes & Dolls 55, 155

Toddles 226, 227

Toddles Gretel 226

Toddles Aviator 226

Toonga from the Congo 225

Topsy 57

Topsy Turvy 154

Toy Tinkers 174

Toylander 81

Tramp 39

Trolley Car (Reed) 222

Trudy 189

Twistum Toy Factory 226

Umbriago 39

Uncle Sam 188, 196

Uneeda Kid 89

Unmarked Dolls & Toys 55, 56, 59, 180-197

Vanitie 13, 22

Virginia Graves 226

Vogue Dolls 226, 227

WAC Doll 202

Warner Brothers 106

Wee Patsy 70, 74

Wee Willie Winkie 93

Wendy-Ann 154

Wimpy 102

Woodstock 218

Zebra 165

ABOUT THE AUTHOR
MICHELE ANN KARL

Michele Karl attended Portland State University where she received her degree in business and marketing. A Portland native, she moved to Seattle, Washington, in the early 1980s to work as a sales representative—where she met her husband, Joe. They have two children, Mathew and Angela, and the Karls now reside in Florida.

Michele's work can be found in both local and national publications—including *Arts & Antiques, Antiques and Collectibles Magazine, Toy Trader, Antique Toy World, Aviation Art Magazine,* and various other magazines in the United States and Canada.